Praise for *E of the Heart*™.

(Continued)

More Praise for *Eight Habits of the Heart™ for Educators*

"Clifton Taulbert eloquently captures the heart and soul of those who are called to serve humanity as teachers and leaders, and challenges each of us to be mindful of the enormous responsibility of nurturing our youngest citizens—the future trustees of our communities and our nation."

—Deborah B. Reeve, Deputy Executive Director
National Association of Elementary School Principals

"Taulbert unselfishly offers educators a practical approach to building strong school communities in a time when we are bombarded by demanding legislation, complex theory, and endless assessments for measuring quality learning. Eight Habits takes us on a refreshing, personable, and sensible journey toward school improvement."

—Glenn E. Singleton, Executive Director, Pacific Educational Group
Author of *Courageous Conversations About Race*

"Eight Habits of the Heart for Educators *is well suited for new as well as seasoned administrators looking to improve student achievement. New teacher mentoring programs would be an ideal place for many of the suggested activities. Weaving in the life experiences of the author creates interest and provides the reader with a sense that putting the habits in place is very possible."*

—Kay Lovelace Taylor, Principal Associate, KLT & Associates

"Clifton Taulbert's eight habits of the heart, combined with his poignant stories, bring to life the all-important notion of building community in school. If only our political leaders and other would-be reformers would take heed, our children and this society would be immeasurably better off."

—Eric Schaps, President Developmental Studies Center

"This volume is a remarkable and compelling testimonial to the potential power of what Clifton Taulbert calls the 'eight habits of the heart' to transform our system of education and our society.

"Nobody is better qualified to write of this, for his own life provides an incredible example of how these habits enabled him to overcome the poverty and deprivation of his youth in the Mississippi Delta in a time of racial segregation.

"Now with infinitely more opportunities than Taulbert had to build a fulfilling and productive life, a new young generation, as well as their parents and teachers, can gain a special insight into what meaningful learning and living are all about.

"This is a book that carries a series of simple but very profound messages for every one of us who desires to build a better life for ourselves and a more stable and fulfilling future for our society."

—William F. Winter, Former Governor of Mississippi
Watkins Ludlam Winter & Stennis, P.A.

Clifton L. Taulbert

Eight Habits of the Heart™
for Educators

**Building Strong
School Communities
Through Timeless Values**

CORWIN PRESS
A SAGE Publications Company
Thousand Oaks, California

For information:

Corwin Press
A Sage Publications Company
2455 Teller Road
Thousand Oaks, California 91320
www.corwinpress.com

Sage Publications Ltd.
1 Oliver's Yard
55 City Road
London EC1Y 1SP
United Kingdom

Sage Publications India Pvt. Ltd.
B-42, Panchsheel Enclave
Post Box 4109
New Delhi 110 017 India

Printed in the United States of America

Library of Congress Cataloging-in-Publication Data

Taulbert, Clifton L.
Eight habits of the heart™ for educators: Building strong school communities through timeless values / Clifton L. Taulbert.
    p. cm.
Includes index.
ISBN 978-1-4129-2630-0 (cloth)—ISBN 978-1-4129-2631-7 (pbk.)
    1. Moral education—United States. 2. Community and school—United States. 3. African Americans—United States—Conduct of life. 4. Conduct of life. I. Title.
LC311.T38 2006
370.11′4—dc22
2005029175
SBENa 7524973 4-24-2015
This book is printed on acid-free paper.

07   08   09   10   10   9   8   7   6   5   4   3

Acquisitions Editor:	Rachel Livsey
Editorial Assistant:	Phyllis Cappello
Production Editor:	Melanie Birdsall
Typesetter:	C&M Digitals (P) Ltd.
Copyeditor:	Cate Huisman
Proofreader:	Cheryl Rivard
Indexer:	Michael Ferreira
Cover Designer:	Lisa Miller

Contents

Preface

Today's educators seem to face almost insurmountable odds. Parents demand more, but they are not always in the forefront of participating in the schools their children attend. Vast amounts of legislation from the government, often specifying the details of what constitutes "a good education," are mounting, but educators still remain the resource to implement and follow through. Student behavior in some instances has become a menace to both the teaching and the learning processes. And as new Americans arrive from every corner of the world, our schools face a growing range of social and cultural issues, along with those created by persistent inequities in our national fabric. The educational landscape is changing at a blistering rate—almost as fast as knowledge itself is growing.

Despite all of these challenges, our nation still has high expectations for education—and I'm talking about the expectations of children, parents, caring neighbors, and the communities in which they live. We have a historical memory of educational excellence, a recollection of the historical partnership of educator, parent, and community that propelled America into a place of world prominence. But alongside this, we have a sense that the foundations of American education are disintegrating and in need of repair.

As educators become concerned about their livelihood—cost-of-living increases outpace income—and personal well-being, some are reexamining their career choice. Shortages exist in the ranks of educators, and this is especially true among men. Only in remote areas of the country where education still remains a major employer are we likely to find equal numbers of men and women in teaching jobs. Education was once considered a high and noble calling; today, many see teaching and related work as "just a job," something to bring in money while they look for a more rewarding profession. As president of the Building Community Institute and a lecturer and workshop leader for educators throughout America and around the world, I see and hear firsthand the conversations of frustration among many of our educators. We all know something is missing.

It's not just that education has gotten tougher. Being a good educator has always been tough. I went to school in Glen Allan, Mississippi, a small community of field hands, maids, and tractor drivers, the folks I've come to call "the porch people." Living in the Mississippi Delta during the era of legal segregation, the teachers and the adults I met every day faced daunting challenges, but somehow, they were able to look beyond the challenges brought on by the system of separate-but-equal. Legal segregation lost much of its momentum within our classrooms, and it was educators who made this so, instilling within us a sense of pride and promising us a future that was still being defined. Our families, standing on their front porches, sent us out to face the future; our teachers, standing at the doors of our schools, welcomed us inside and helped prepare us for that future. Without their unselfish hearts and hands helping me along in my life, this book would not be possible. In many ways, they helped to prepare me for this day.

In some respects, however, this book was born not in the Glen Allan of my youth but decades later and up the road a ways in Tupelo, Mississippi, where I was invited to speak at an annual fundraiser for a social and educational club serving the community's boys and girls. I remember the night vividly. When we arrived, the place was already packed with ordinary people of both races and a good number of representatives from the business community. The young people who would benefit from the evening's charitable effort were looking their best, uniformed in matching T-shirts and southern smiles.

Before dinner, I spent some time talking to the guests, many of whom were in leadership positions, as they shared with me the various backgrounds, social behavior problems, and living environments of each child, offering detailed data and demographics on each and every one. I got a clear picture of where these youngsters had come from, and I saw that though many years had passed, their young lives were not that different from my own childhood. What troubled me is that everyone was so busy telling me where these kids *came from* no one bothered to talk about *who they could become,* or who they really were in the scheme of life.

Although the circumstances of my life had been far worse than what many of those youth experienced, no one in my environment had focused on the demographics and hardships of my situation as a description of me. Instead, the people around me offered an entirely different picture of who I was; they made up a community that had my future at its center. At that moment, I had an epiphany: My relatives, teachers, and others saw all my potential and all that I could become. They kept before me the positive picture that still drives my life today.

Although I was a grown man standing in Tupelo, Mississippi, I was emotionally in the first grade again, standing in the presence of my teacher, whom we all called Miss Mary Maxey, following southern usage, even though she was married to Mr. Joe. She paid no attention to our living and social conditions. Rather, she welcomed us into her first-grade classroom as if we were the sons and daughters of kings and presidents. Miss Maxey and all the others I met in that school wanted us—the children of field hands, maids, and tractor drivers—to have a different and positive view of ourselves. One night, she gathered a few of us in a clearing outside the wooden frame building that was her first schoolhouse and pointed to the starlit heavens. Miss Maxey told us to remember that we were among the stars—bright, gifted, and shining—even in the daylight when the sun's brightness overshadowed the light from the stars. She said the stars were constantly shining, and she expected no less from us. Learning was to be our constant pursuit wherever we were.

As I remembered those old days, I understood that the success of the Tupelo social club would depend not just on our ability to raise money or assess demographic data but on our success in getting educators and supporting adults to make a commitment to this positive view of their youngsters' potential and to building a community where their students could thrive. A good school community required more than bricks and mortar when I was growing up, and today, it still does.

Once I had this new emotionally charged picture of the Tupelo youngsters etched in my mind, the notes I has prepared were no longer of value. I crumpled them up and threw them away. When the dinner was over and it was time for me to speak, I walked to the front of the room, but not to the podium. I stood very close to the first row of tables, looking closely into the eyes of each child present, and the children's eyes met mine. I hesitated, but only for a moment, and then I began by inviting the youngsters to stand. I asked the audience if they had a clear picture of just who these young people were. I could hear them repeating what they had told me earlier: "These are the children from the other side of town, children from broken homes or children from our projects." That was all true, but there was a greater truth— one that I had experienced as a child.

"Tonight, these youth are much more than children we have rescued," I told the group. "We are privileged to be with them. I know clearly who they are. They are the future trustees of our communities. How we view them and what we expect from them will make all the difference in how they view themselves and how they welcome and meet the awesome tasks ahead of them. It will make all the difference in the future of our nation."

It seems to me that this is what's missing from our schools today: a positive vision of our students to drive our efforts and the courage to build the kind of community that will make the most of their potential. I left Tupelo determined to use my voice to make sure that we do not, through our conversations, perspectives, and loads of social data, negatively brand our children. Rather, we must view all of our students as the future trustees of our communities and of our country. I have challenged adults I've met throughout America—parents, caretakers, and educators—to adopt this vision and never to underestimate our responsibility to the youngsters who pass through our care. This is especially important for many of our inner-city students, who may be in great need of emotional support.

In this book, I extend that challenge to my readers, to teachers and others involved in educating our youngsters. Looking around at your students' home lives, you may wonder if they're up to the task of being our community's trustees, but I challenge you to set their sights on a future only they can create, a future beyond peeling plaster and police sirens. Students in places that share the poverty and disadvantage, even discrimination, of the rural Mississippi town where I grew up must embrace their humanity and discover the gifts that live within them.

Just as Miss Maxey and my other teachers had this positive "inside" picture of me, educators throughout America—from the highest levels of our government to the last staff person hired at the elementary school in Douglas, Arizona—can do enormous good if they have the same kind of picture of the students in their schools. I now fully understand that I was fortunate to have grown up in that time and place, in a community of porch people. And because of committed educators, today's youth will be able to say that their educational experience was enriched. Educators, thank you for continuing this honorable tradition of keeping students focused on a future that includes them.

This book is for you, my educator benefactor and friend. It's about your long-standing unique role in the life of young people. It's about building solid relationships among your peers for the benefit of students. It's about leadership and what it means to set out purposely to bring others along, placing a high value on collaboration. This book is about the heartbeat of education, building community. School communities provide the necessary infrastructure of relationships at all levels, a foundational place where all educational initiatives can take root and grow.

Chapter 1 focuses on what community looks like in schools and how educators can go about the building process, establishing this very necessary foundation of relationships to support important initiatives such as civic education, character education, and of course service learning—all of these can flourish in the presence of good community. In Chapter 2, I describe "the human touch," the acts of unselfishness that meant so much to me during my school years. In these two chapters, readers will see how they can lay a foundation for academic excellence by creating a community in which personal unselfishness and commitment to students drive the educational agenda. In Chapter 3, I describe how I distilled from my youthful experiences the Eight Habits of the Heart, and the following chapters discuss each in turn. By embracing these eight principles, which I now know to be timeless and universal, educators can develop personal operational strategies for building and sustaining the community *they* envision as critical to the teaching and learning process.

Please keep in mind that the intention of this book is not to provide detailed instructions, to-do lists, and activity handouts that can be used to replicate particular outcomes. In Chapters 3 through 10, you will find some questions to prompt your reflection or provoke group discussion. The chapters also include some "opportunities" to implement the Eight Habits in your own school situation, some strategies other educators have proposed, and vignettes of educators I've met who embodied one of these habits in a particular time and place. The idea, however, is not to direct your activity but to fire your imagination. I hope each of you will consider the possibilities.

The community my teachers and elders built and the timeless and universal principles they practiced are a guiding star, not a template. Think about the Eight Habits of the Heart—Nurturing Attitude, Responsibility, Dependability, Friendship, Brotherhood, High Expectations, Courage, and Hope—and make them your very own as you set out to expand upon this noble tradition of excellence: building a community in which students can become the best and brightest people their skills and talents permit.

After all, they are the future trustees of their communities and our country.

Acknowledgments

This book would have not been possible had I not encountered so many wonderful people along the way. I want to thank Dr. Kevin Ryan and Dr. Karen Bohlin, formerly with Boston University's Center for the Advancement of Ethics and Character, for including me as a professor in a summer academy held for the South Carolina Department of Education. I especially thank Camille Nairn and Rebecca Cupstid with South Carolina's Department of Education for making sure that their educators were part of my journey. I thank Dr. Kathy Paget of the University of South Carolina for her evaluation process, and Dr. Mili Pierce, formerly head of the Harvard Principals' Center, for embracing the concept of building community within schools as an academic imperative and including me among her guest professors. Many educators around the world would not have known about the Eight Habits of the Heart had it not been for Mary Anne Haas with the American International Schools. She introduced me and our concepts to Central America, Europe, and other parts of the world.

I also thank Robb Clouse with Corwin Press for tracking me down and listening to my lectures and always reminding me that I had something of value to say to educators. Rachel Livsey, my editor, found a way to eliminate excessive and redundant southern chatter so that my message could shine through. Thank you very much. Special thanks to Dr. Deborah Reeve, Dr. Cheryl Riggins, and Margaret Evans, staff persons with the National Association of Elementary School Principals, for their early and constant support of the Eight Habits of the Heart. And to Oklahoma educators Dr. Belinda McCharen, Ms. Juanita Williams,

Dr. Mary Merritt, Dr. Kirby Lehman, and so many others, thank you sincerely for your support and welcome into the world of primary and secondary education. And last but not least, I thank my staff at The Building Community Institute; Douglas Decker, my assistant; and my wife, Barbara, for supporting me in this exciting journey. There are so many others I wish to thank, and some of you will find your names and our conversations sprinkled throughout the book. And yes, thank you, Miss Maxey, my first-grade teacher, for helping me to feel welcomed on my first day so long ago.

The contributions of the following reviewers are gratefully acknowledged:

Diane Barone
Professor of Literacy Studies
University of Nevada, Reno
Reno, NV

Kay Lovelace Taylor
Principal Associate
KLT & Associates
Scottsdale, AZ

Douglas Fisher
Professor of Teacher Education
San Diego State University
San Diego, CA

John C. Hughes
Principal
Public School 48
The Joseph R. Drake School
Bronx, NY

About the Author

Clifton L. Taulbert, president and founder of The Building Community Institute, is the author of the award-winning *Once Upon a Time When We Were Colored*, the Pulitzer-nominated *The Last Train North*, and the internationally acclaimed *Eight Habits of the Heart*. Now in *Eight Habits of the Heart for Educators*, Taulbert takes us further into the world of his youth—the Mississippi Delta and the many educators who through their unselfishness built community for him and countless thousands when teaching and learning were taking place in a largely segregated world.

He has served as a guest professor at Harvard University's Principals' Center, Boston University's Center for the Advancement of Ethics and Character Summer Academies, the United States Air Force Academy, and the American International Schools Conference, and serves as an adjunct professor at the Federal Executive Institute. A frequent presenter, Taulbert has served as the keynote speaker at meetings of the National Association of Elementary School Principals, the National Middle School Association, the National School Board Association, and the National Alliance of Black School Educators. Among his many awards and recognitions are the Richard Wright Annual Literary Award for Excellence, the National Jewish Humanitarian of the Year Award, and an NAACP Image Award for his book *Once Upon a Time When We Were Colored*, hailed as an outstanding contribution to literature.

Taulbert is also a board member of the National Character Education Partnership and is on the Board of Trustees of Tulsa University.

Clifton Taulbert is recognized internationally as a thought leader on the critical issue of community as a valuable asset for this century. He was on CNN's *Millennium Minute for Community* and has carried this important message around the world through lectures, forums, and curriculums. For this author and lecturer, community is a dynamic process, one in which each of us can be part. Taulbert's timeless and universal concepts have also become part of the Ninth House e-learning company's international offerings, partnering him with such notable e-learning professors as Tom Peters, Ken Blanchard, and Peter Senge. Through his Eight Habits of the Heart, he provides the framework to challenge our thinking and direct our actions—personal actions that will ensure the presence of RAI . . . Respect, Affirmation, and Inclusion—within our personal space and within our professional places.

Taulbert currently lives in Tulsa, Oklahoma, where he shares his life with his wife Barbara. They both share the joy of their adult son Marshall Danzy Taulbert.

This book, Eight Habits of the Heart for Educators,
is dedicated to the memory of one of
the Mississippi Delta's great educators,

my mother,
Mary Morgan Taulbert,

who, through the span of her life,
was a cotton fieldworker,
a plantation school teacher, and a maid,
and ended her educational career as the successful
Director of Washington County's Yates Head-Start Center,

and to all those others
who embrace this noble profession.

CHAPTER 1

Building Community . . .
The Foundation for Excellence

*No society can remain vital or even survive
without a reasonable base of shared values.
Where community exists, it confers upon its
members, identity, a sense of belonging, a measure
of security. A community has the power to motivate
its members to exceptional performance. Community
can set standards of expectations for the individual
and provide the climate in which great things happen.*

—JOHN W. GARDNER, FORMER
PROFESSOR, STANFORD UNIVERSITY

Building community is the foundation for any successful educational journey. Academic initiatives and educational resources of every kind will have little impact until the framework for building community is established. In his remarks above, John W. Gardner, who was U.S. Secretary of Health, Education, and Welfare during the civil rights movement, offers us an insightful look at what happens when community is in place: All members feel safe and encouraged to do—and be—their very best, both individually and together.

Today, the concept of building community in schools is rather widespread, but real school communities are far less commonplace. We all know the value of community. Recently, however, we have mistakenly thought that community would "happen" automatically while we gave our time and attention to the applications of systems and programs. And in so thinking, we removed ourselves from this very important field of play. Drs. Thomas Lickona and Marvin Berkowitz, character education research specialists, tell me that caring environments are just as essential to learning in the 21st century as they were when I was a boy growing up in Glen Allan, Mississippi. This is not to downplay the importance of technology to the learning process but rather to play up the importance of our continued personal role in ensuring the presence of good community in our schools and on our playgrounds.

Although the title of this book is *Eight Habits of the Heart for Educators,* as I see it, building a school community is the master plan for our project. If we take the school community as our blueprint, then the Eight Habits of the Heart—behaviors I found modeled in the Mississippi Delta community where I grew up—are the construction materials:

Nurturing Attitude

Responsibility

Dependability

Friendship

Brotherhood

High Expectations

Courage

Hope

They're great building blocks, but we may not achieve the result we want unless we have a blueprint. Obviously, we also need the glue or mortar, if you like, to assemble the materials, and to me, the glue is the spirit of unselfishness that was pervasive in the environment of my youth and in the schools I attended, a spirit that remains available in these times.

So before we talk about the Eight Habits in detail, it seems to me, we should have an idea in our heads of where we're going and the general direction we need to head in order to get there. In this chapter, we'll take a close look at what a school community looks like: What do you need to turn your school into a community where not only students but educators, too, will thrive? Then, in Chapter 2, we turn to unselfishness—what I call "the human touch"—and how that can be a force to bring us together. Finally, in Chapter 3, I'll tell you how the Eight Habits of the Heart came to be and why I think the lessons I learned on the Mississippi Delta so long ago can help you transform your schools. In each chapter of this book, you'll find some opportunities to participate in the project of building community at your school. I hope you'll find them useful.

The core of this book is based on my experiences in Glen Allan, Mississippi, in the 1950s. Back then, educators seemed to know instinctively just how to create a community in which their students could thrive. They knew who their students were, and our names constituted more than an attendance roll. Our teachers identified with our lives. They made it a point to know our families, and parents were welcomed visitors within our school. In spite of negative remarks others may have made about us—those who didn't care to know us—our teachers knew we had the capabilities to become great people, and their lesson plans and daily conversations reflected their vision for our future.

It was a time when *service learning*—doing for others—was commonplace, and learning about the nation in which we lived was expected and welcomed. Our teachers didn't call it "character education," but their expectations for good behavior were everywhere. They'd often say, "Find you a good pattern and cut your life out by it." Looking back, I can honestly say that it was indeed a visionary time, although it was also marked by a social system that had not yet matured to fully embrace our shared humanity. However, my schoolmates and I were fortunate because of educators who continued to plan for a great future. Miss Maxey, my first-grade teacher, started the process for me. Let me tell you a little about the day I met her.

✐ From the Front Porch

School started in early September in the 1950s, and the sun was still hot in the Mississippi Delta while the humidity, as always, showered us like rain. For the first time, I was facing the monumental task of leaving the safety and comfort of my great-grandparents' home for my very first day at school. My great-grandparents, Poppa Joe and Mama Pearl, were clearly excited about my adventure, but their enthusiasm had not yet trickled down to me.

I didn't want to go. I might have stayed all day in my small bedroom, but the smell of cured ham gently led me out to the sunporch where both my great-grandparents were waiting with smiles. As soon as I had eaten my breakfast—not only Poppa's cured ham, but grits, hot biscuits, and molasses—Mama Pearl eagerly led me to her bedroom, where she pointed out my new clothes laid out on the bed: long blue jeans, a long-sleeved plaid shirt, and, worst of all, new high-top shoes. Mama Pearl stood beaming by the foot of the iron bed. Poppa yelled from the sunporch, "Boy, you like your new stuff?" Mama Pearl answered for me, "Sure he does."

I said nothing. It was hot, and all I could see were winter clothes. At that moment, the world that I had known all my young life ended. I was afraid. School was for the big children, not for me. Nevertheless, I got dressed, and Mama Pearl and I set out for school. As I walked slowly behind her, Mama Pearl kept calling out to me to run and catch up. Inevitably, I did. With the Glen Allan "Colored School" in sight, Mama Pearl walked even faster, so excited you'd have thought *she* was going to school. She was full of talk about what she saw, and when she got to the school, she immediately grabbed my hand and walked me to the teacher, who was standing in the front door with the biggest smile I'd ever seen.

Miss Maxey, the teacher, welcomed Mama Pearl and me and reached out and shook my hand. "Go on in. Go on in," Mama Pearl kept saying, so I did. Once I was inside, Miss Maxey pointed out cousins and friends on the playground and showed me where I would be sitting, right by the big window. And then she gave me my very own book and talked with me about how much fun learning would be. She worked her teacher magic on me, and my fear began to go away.

On my first day of school, I left a place where I was safe and well loved—a little fearfully, I'll admit—for another place where I would be safe and well loved. Miss Maxey welcomed me inside, showed me that people I knew were already there, gave me my own place, and spoke to me—one to one—about all the interesting things we would be doing together. Poppa Joe, Mama Pearl, and Miss Maxey built *community* for me, a secure and welcoming world where I could set my fears aside and think beyond the only life I had known.

I grew up in a world that was far less than perfect. In an era of segregated education, what were then referred to as "colored schools" had secondhand books; their students weren't invited to participate in library events, and we were sometimes called names by those in authority; some of us had to leave school to work whenever the cotton farmers came for us. But these negative influences were held at bay because the caring community would have it no other way. Our teachers paid no heed to Jim Crow, the legal and social laws that were designed to foster thoughts of inferiority. The teachers were guided by their vision of who we were and who we could become. Our teachers stretched our imagination, protected us in our uncertain world, and set us out on a course to achieve great things. Educators can have no higher goals.

> How can you make your students feel welcome in your school?
>
> How can you boost your students' view of themselves?
>
> How can you protect your students from today's problems?

Today, there are still many students who need a new and positive view of themselves—and educators who can help them achieve this vision. Educators still know how important it is for students to have their minds fully engaged if they are to grasp the lessons and to make the connections between what they're learning and their daily lives, to say nothing of their future plans. You must set out with the intention of building an environment essential to growing and developing students' lives in the most positive manner possible. The process of doing so will affect your work as educators, and the academic returns for your students will be worth your commitment of time, energy, resources, and creativity.

In addition, as you build a community for your students, they will see a model that they, too, can use to build community among their peers. Positive behavior and healthy relationships will develop among your students as they become engaged in the principles required to build community. Being fully engaged can be impeded by numerous barriers and roadblocks: feeling insecure, being bullied, and having low self-esteem, as well as reading and comprehension challenges, medical conditions, and the lack of support from a parent or caregiver. A good caring community provides a safe place for honest communication, the first step in eliminating or reducing the roadblocks to full engagement.

> *What possibilities do you see in the faces of your students?*
>
> *How do you ignore the negativity surrounding many of their lives?*
>
> *How do you propose to make each student in your class feel?*

But how do we get there from here? This remains the challenge. It's not easy to focus on building community when the school day presents so many demands if educators are to meet local, state, and federal requirements. Community in schools will not show up on its own, however. You must define the community you want for your classroom and your school; this is a critical first step toward understanding what you will need to do to build and maintain it.

As an educator, you have the lead role. You are the one out front with the title, the position, and the influence. Community building can start with you and your willingness to put forth the effort on a daily basis in spite of all the other challenges you face. But you do have help, and much of it will come from your fellow educators. You can start by asking them to join with you in imagining a new school community and in listing all the things they believe are needed—on a personal level—to make that dream come true.

In educator workshops I hold around the country, participants are asked to come up with a personal definition of a productive caring school community and then—the tough part—to create one group definition from their individual input. At first, they appear reluctant to give up any part of their individual definition. But left with little choice, they soon begin to talk among themselves, find common ground, and develop a group definition of community that reflects all their input. Here's one group's list:

In an Ideal School Community . . .

- There is consistent opportunity to invite, nurture, achieve, and reach full potential respectfully.
- Everyone respects others, fosters growth, and appreciates diversity while being nurturers and lifelong learners.
- There is an eager exchange of thought, where values and opinions are respected, modeled, and accepted.
- Diverse groups share goals, knowledge, and opportunity with support and encouragement from each other.
- Everyone demonstrates respect and cooperation, providing for interdependence among the members, while allowing for uniqueness and creativity.
- Members foster intrinsic motivation in an accepting and nurturing environment—one that values excellence and encourages all to achieve their maximum potential.

In our workshops, this exercise does several things. First, it points out that educators all have their own ideas of what a good community should look like. Second, by having to create a group definition, the participants recognize the value of communication and discover that one mosaic can be created from many thoughts—an ideal that now bears all their signatures. This exercise also bonds educators who may not have known each other before the workshop, and afterward, I notice a freer flow of information among them. They ask questions of each other, and they laugh and touch each other. By defining community together, they also discover values they have in common.

I have also noticed that many of the group definitions look the same, although they come from different sets of educators from different parts of the country and the world. If providing the best for children is at the center of their thinking, it doesn't matter if educators are from Alaska, Central America, South Carolina, or South Dakota—they all seem to think along the same lines.

Opportunity to Build Community in Your School

- Personally define your ideal teaching/learning community—using twelve words or less.
- Invite another educator or two to join you by creating their personal definitions of community.
- Once you have more than one definition, create a group definition.

Can you live with and celebrate the new definition?

Once the ideal community is defined, the next steps are vastly important. How do you bring the ideal to life? How do you move this task beyond intellectual conversations? What will be required of each individual educator? What tools will you use? How can you do this in spite of the obstacles or barriers in your way?

Educators Just Like You . . . Building a School Community

Dr. Delores Saunders, a member of the Department of Defense Educational Administration team in Frankfurt, Germany, and most recently a former president of the National Alliance of Black School Educators, asked me to help them build community within the military schools in Europe, parts of Asia, and Central America. She especially wanted teachers to understand that community could not be left to chance. Educators had a dual responsibility not only to teach the required curriculum but to build the necessary climate for that curriculum's success. Dr. Vicki Lake, now a professor at Florida State University, was assigned to work with me.

As Dr. Lake remembers those days,

> Four of us worked for two weeks that summer to create this curriculum. The next school year we took the show on the road, so to speak, and fine-tuned the faculty module. Our premise was to start with the adults in the school, create a caring community, then come back and work with individual classrooms.

Workshops were designed. Training took place and the idea of building community within school became a topic of priority. Over time, we were all able to see the impact of the community being built, as educators first embraced each other and then reached out to parents, staff, and the community, all for the benefit of the children. The future of the children became the center of focus as it was in Glen Allan, Mississippi, when I grew up. Specific side benefits of impacting student behavior and character development also emerged as this building community curriculum was put in place. I began to see that when community exists within schools, students dream; grades improve and so does behavior. This last item—discipline—was a particular interest of Dr. Lake:

> I had always struggled with the dichotomy of the rewards-and-punishment classroom management system and my obligation and duty toward young children to empower them by teaching and modeling pro-social skills. My school wanted me to use a discipline model that starts with a warning, name on the board, loss of recess or time out, etc. . . . almost every classroom uses this system. It is not a bad system, but it was not and is not congruent with my philosophy of children or teaching.
>
> How could I really teach character traits, model them, and expect children to practice them in an environment that focused on punishment? It did not work for me. My last few years in the classroom,

I threw out assertive discipline and focused on cooperative leaning with specific attention to teaching pro-social skills or character traits.

Many of the skills Vicki Lake talks about would find a comfortable home somewhere in the Eight Habits of the Heart. It's heartwarming to know that the notion of building community continues to move beyond the small schools of the Mississippi Delta where I first experienced it.

CHAPTER 2

Building Community . . .
The Human Touch

*Classroom teachers give young people
what they sometimes get nowhere else in
society—a sense that they have promise, that
they have talents, that they are special. If you're
a young person who is not quite sure that you are
welcome in this society, one of the most important
people in your life could be a teacher who accepts you.*

—PARKER J. PALMER

The community I encountered as a child was characterized by individual acts of unselfishness—"the human touch" that makes "community" real. Without those daily acts of personal unselfishness from Poppa, Mama Ponk, Uncle Cleve, Miss Florence, and my teachers—acts that benefited me and acts I saw that benefited others—my life experience would have been drastically different. Their actions provided the warmth, the friendship, the leadership, the sharing of knowledge, the discipline, the shelter, the conversation, the emotional support, and the feelings of security I needed as a child and still need today. Their actions were the gifts inside the house, inside the classroom, and on the playground; the gifts that showed up on the front porch; and, of course, the gifts that set our school apart. I would later learn that *community* is just a word without the unselfishness that infuses it with life.

My experience over the years is that unselfishness—"the human touch"—also lies at the heart of what the students and educators who make up school communities want and need. I use the term *touch* because I want educators to understand that the community they define and seek to build requires "people to people" interaction, both physically and emotionally. You cannot requisition a good, productive, and fulfilling school community from the district office. A school community must be personally built on a daily basis by both you and your students. That message is at the heart of this book. It's something I learned years ago in Glen Allan.

✺ From the Front Porch

In Glen Allan, front porches were always open and welcoming, not just to family and friends but to strangers walking by. Our neighbors could see us, and we could see them. No barriers separated us from their voices or from their acts. People realized that their visible unselfish behavior could positively influence their children.

Surrounded by barriers, both institutional and embedded social restrictions, these ordinary people living more than a half century ago set out to build community for their children. They understood that we were the trustees of their future, even if they wouldn't have used those words. They were determined and consistent with their unselfish contributions—that made all the difference.

When I was a young student, the touch looked like shared conversations with Miss Ross, the second-grade teacher who always found time to talk about matters outside the classroom. Those conversations broadened our worldview. No matter the rigors of his workday, our elementary school principal, Mr. Moore, always found time to point out the value of reading and to point us to the small library as a destination.

When I entered high school, Mr. Givhan, our math teacher, wanted every one of us to excel in algebra and put in place peer mentoring, though it was not called that at the time. He wanted all of us to make A's. Staying after class to provide extra help was commonplace with him as it was with Miss Jackson, our science teacher. She knew that the science lab was foreign to many of us and went out of her way to humanize biology and to help us see beyond our limited world. As a student, I needed both their professional and caring voices. Students still need both today.

In the Mississippi Delta, I experienced some level of daily unselfishness from all my teachers. I believe it is really the touch—our unselfish acts—that define good community in every age and will build the school culture of your dreams. What does "the human touch" look like in your school community? What acts of unselfishness would educators like to see on the part of their leaders? How would they like to be treated by their peers?

We regularly put those questions to educators in workshops all over the country. Here's what happened when I met with some educators from South Dakota. The audience consisted of more than 100 adults, but none that looked like me. Although I wondered whether the stories of my porch people from the Mississippi Delta would work in the prairies of South Dakota, the workshop participants soon relaxed, settled back, and joined me on this journey.

As they moved through the workshop, the educators engaged in exercises to define community and then to flesh out what they would need from their leadership and from among themselves to ensure "the touch" within that community. We always ask our workshop participants to step out, to be visionary and focused when listing their expectations of others. It's always easier to articulate your expectations of others than to focus on what is required of you—just keep in mind that others will expect the same of you. Here's what educators said they needed from school leaders:

Unselfish Acts Educators Want From Leadership

- Enforce rules fairly.
- Take recess duty.
- Step into the classroom to visit more often.
- Ask staff members about their families.
- Model what you expect of others—don't just list your expectations.
- Visit each building at least once a week to encourage the teachers and to show your interest in the students.
- Say "good morning" and be polite; we are, after all, part of the same team.
- Give advice on how to improve my classroom after having visited over a period of time.
- Don't judge my work unless you have seen it.
- Value my opinion by honestly listening to what I have to say and acknowledging my contribution to the success of the school.
- Offer positive advice to correct a situation or to keep a negative one from happening.
- Treat teacher union representatives with respect for their voluntary jobs; such a commitment will be beneficial for all concerned.

While the exact elements may vary from one workshop to another, we've found that most lists reflect a need for respect, affirmation, and inclusion. It seems as if the educators are saying to leadership, "We've come together for the same purpose, to educate our children for their future. We function best when you recognize and celebrate our shared humanity. Together, we can create the ideal environment for learning success. Mutual respect is essential."

We also ask educators to list the unselfish behaviors they need from each other to complement what they feel they need from leadership. Here's what the response was in South Dakota:

Unselfish Acts Educators Want From Each Other

- Listen to each other with open minds; we all have different opinions and views.
- Eat lunch with a different coworker each day to create broad relationships.
- Treat all colleagues with respect even if you don't agree; students will observe this.
- Communicate with each other frequently, even when there are no problems to solve.
- Say "good morning" to each other with a smile and really mean it.
- Take the time to know each other on a personal level beyond the classroom.
- Always tell the truth even if it means a backlash for you.
- Trust each other's judgment as we work on projects together; we are professionals.
- Share student information with each other when appropriate.

Again, the responses provided by South Dakota educators may not include everything you need for an ideal school community, but if this wish list were taken to heart, embraced, and lived out, you would be well on your way.

Opportunity to Build
Unselfishness in Your School: Educators

List three specific unselfish acts you want from each designated group to build the school community you envision.

- Principal or superintendent (leadership)
- Other teachers
- Students
- Parents or caregiver(s)

    Share your list and discuss it with others. Look for the common concerns and for new thoughts. Discuss ways to elicit the unselfishness you want from others.

    Now let's look at the thinking among the most important members of the school community: your students. After all, students are the intended focus of our efforts to build community within their schools. What do they think? What do they want? It's important to incorporate their opinions into our plans to build a school community, just as it's important to ensure that they are heard in the daily life of our schools. Soliciting student opinions is rarely part of the lesson plan, so educators besieged by the need to meet standards and other requirements may find it easy to ignore the thoughts and opinions of their students.

At an international youth workshop conducted in San José, Costa Rica, we had an opportunity to meet with Central American students and American students whose parents were employed in Central America—students of varied social and economic backgrounds. We asked what they thought about unselfishness and what they hoped to receive from the adults who were building community for them. Here's what they said:

Unselfish Acts Students Want From Educators

- Take time to talk with us.
- Act wisely in any situation; don't jump to decisions too quickly.
- Be patient when we do something wrong; we are still learning.
- Be open-minded and slow to reject our ideas.
- Practice humility.
- Understand that we also have a lot to do, even if we are students.
- Respect our privacy.
- Recognize our good aspects and accomplishments in front of our peers.
- Be a real person; do not be superficial.
- Respect us as people, and don't put us down.
- Believe in our potential, even if it's not always apparent.
- Accept and acknowledge that adults make mistakes, too.

Then, we asked the students to give some thought to what they needed from each other so that their ideal school community would function successfully.

Unselfish Acts Students Want From Each Other

- Act courteously among ourselves.
- Be persistent in the hardest times.
- Do not create cliques.
- When you sign up, show up.
- Take advantage of differences by uniting around issues we have in common.
- Communicate with everyone, including those whose social class is different from yours.
- See educators not as employees but as possible friends.
- Do not criticize or make fun of others.
- Do not be driven by envy; develop true friendship.
- Be brave enough to say when something is wrong.
- Be honest; have few false attitudes.

I was struck with how many of the students' responses correlated with those from the adult workshops. It seems as if these qualities reflect universal needs, what is essential for both students and adults to provide the basis for the type of community they wish to *develop* and, most important, to *cultivate*.

Opportunity to Build
Unselfishness in Your School: Students

- Have your students define their ideal school community.
- Ask them to list what they need from their peers to create their ideal.
- Pick the top five or ten unselfish actions, and make them into a poster.
- Display the poster for referral during the school year.

As a student attending the International Youth Conference in Central America said—and I agree— "A little unselfishness can go a long ways." A good, productive, and caring school community will always be characterized by involvement: "the touch" that students still need to encounter. In a positive and caring community, students' negative or nonproductive views are changed. The key is caring. When we care, acting to benefit others comes naturally. These concepts of "the touch" are not exclusive to the Mississippi Delta; you can bring them into your school communities, as you set out to create or recapture the unselfishness you experienced or wished for yourself. Your students will benefit, as I did.

Opportunity to Build Community in Your School

One of the great educators of the recent century was Dr. Mary McLeod Bethune, known as the great conversationalist. Rather than having ideas, visions, or challenges, she chose to create forums for conversation, and in so doing left an incredible legacy of education. Following her lead, have conversations with your fellow educators.

Waving from your desk to a fellow educator who passes by is not conversation. Nodding at each other in the hall or waving at each other across the parking lot is a good gesture but not a great conversation. The teachers' lounge is a good place to initiate great conversations. When you talk among yourselves, you also discover your common humanity: Imaginary walls are penetrated, honest assessments are shared, commonalities are discovered, and yes, possibilities emerge that might not have surfaced otherwise.

CHAPTER 3

Building Community . . .
Life Lessons From the
Mississippi Delta

*What the best and wisest parent wants
for his own child, that must the community
want for all its children. Any other ideal
for our schools is narrow and unlovely;
acted upon, it destroys our democracy.*

—JOHN DEWEY

Now that we have seen the importance of a school community and looked at how "the human touch" might answer the needs of the students and educators, I'd like to return with you to the Mississippi Delta where I grew up. We've talked a bit about my great-grandparents, Poppa Joe and Mama Pearl, and about my first-grade teacher, Miss Maxey. It's time to tell you a bit more about Glen Allan and how the people there gave me a gift I now call the Eight Habits of the Heart.

❧ From the Front Porch

At my elementary school in Glen Allan, everyone seemed to know that the job of educating children was their greatest priority, from Mr. Moore, the principal, to Miss Bootsie, the bus driver, Miss Carrie, the cook, and Mr. Powell, the janitor. Teachers, parents, and school staff also seemed to realize that educating their children would ultimately be among their greatest achievements. I call this their benevolent conspiracy.

In the small Glen Allan school community, everyone knew each other. People talked among themselves. They shared their knowledge unselfishly, and the success of one became the joy of all. And we the students saw those important activities of community building and unselfish caring as they took place.

You know, even today, some 50 years later, I still call our janitor "Mr. Powell," and when I think of my educational experience, he is right there along with my teachers and parents. I readily recall Mr. Powell's neat look, his ever-present key ring, and his sense of ownership in our lives. Mr. Powell was more than the clean-up man. He was treated with great respect by the teachers and our principal, and in return, he respected them and became an able member of my education team.

Mr. Powell was one of my teachers; of that I am sure, and here's how. Mr. Powell always followed the rules set by the principal. He parked in his assigned spot. You knew exactly where to find him. He always started out his day neatly dressed. He tipped his cap to the teachers and knew nearly every student by name. He would ask about our grades, and if we were outside of the classroom too long, he'd inquire as to why. From his perspective, learning was taking place on the inside, and we were missing something if we weren't there. He was always present at our morning devotions.

Mr. Powell may have left the reading, writing, and 'rithmetic to Miss Maxey and her fellow teachers, but he offered invaluable lessons in things like Responsibility, Dependability, and a Nurturing Attitude—as well as having High Expectations for each and every one of us.

The builders of my community left for me—and for the next generation and for who knows how many others—a series of rich life lessons. But although I was grateful for the caring education I had received during my time in Glen Allan, it was only ten years ago that I fully understood not just what I had learned but also that these lessons could be applied beyond my time and beyond the narrow boundaries of Glen Allan to assist educators who are charged with the care of other youngsters today.

I was invited to Germany to speak to a group of international educators. When I was asked afterward to develop a learning and training strategy to help them build new educational communities, I had to look no farther than the fields of the Mississippi Delta I had been telling them about. I knew the answers were there. I had seen my teachers not only in school but on their front porches, and I had benefited from their wisdom. I saw community. I felt community. I knew that it evolved in spite of roadblocks—hurdles no lower than the challenges facing educators today.

> Take a minute and think about the schools you attended as a student. Did your teachers and the staff form a community committed to your growth?
>
> Can we retain community building as a high priority in a world defined by bits and bytes and Pentium chips?

As I thought about using the people I had known all my life as the prototype of good community builders, I was at first slightly apprehensive. After all, they were ordinary people—merely field hands, maids, tractor drivers, bus drivers, cooks, preachers, and a sprinkling of teachers. Who they were and how they lived had seemed ordinary and routine to me at the time; now, I saw that the community they built was dynamic and transformational.

So I began to analyze their lives, one by one, examining their routine daily actions for the elements that had enabled me and countless thousands of African Americans to rise beyond physical poverty and mental abuse to become partners in the building and shaping of America. I started with my great-grandfather, the Reverend Joe Young. I looked at Poppa Joe's life from all sides and all angles, and then I began to look at others within the community—other kin, teachers, and just good people, making notes on what was similar and what actions were unique. I paid special attention to the consistency of unselfish efforts.

As a result, I was able to distill my findings—the consistent and intentional unselfishness that showed up in their daily living and in the community they built—into eight powerful, timeless, and universal principles. I call these principles the Eight Habits of the Heart. Through them, I have tried to broaden the application and universality of their intentional unselfishness—giving form and accountability to the look and feel of "the human touch" within our community.

These Eight Habits will help focus your use of time and help you share your knowledge to benefit others. As these habits continue to grow in your life, you'll find your emotions directing your actions, and your students and peers will be touched by the extension of care beyond the workplace into the lives of others. These habits will also give you a view of what we have in common, as they exhort us to encourage others to live beyond imposed limitations. Your commitment to these timeless and universal habits will lead you on a path of seeking truth for yourself and for others as a solid foundation under your school community. And because you are embracing these habits, you will see your life become a window through which others can view a positive picture of their future.

The Eight Habits of the Heart

Nurturing Attitude	A Nurturing Attitude is characterized by unselfish caring, supportiveness, and a willingness to share time.
Responsibility	Responsibility is showing and encouraging a personal commitment to each task.
Dependability	Dependability is being there for others through all the time of their lives, a steady influence that makes tomorrow a welcome event.
Friendship	Friendship is the habit that binds people together when we take pleasure in each other's company, listen, laugh, and share good times and bad.
Brotherhood	Brotherhood is the habit that reaches beyond comfortable relationships to extend a welcome to those who may be different from ourselves.
High Expectations	High Expectations involve believing that others can be successful, telling them so, and praising their accomplishments.
Courage	Courage is standing up and doing the right thing, speaking out on behalf of others, and making a commitment to excellence in the face of adversity or the absence of support.
Hope	Hope is believing in tomorrow—going beyond what we see because we have learned to see with our hearts.

As I present each of these Eight Habits of the Heart in the following chapters, I will share a story from the porch people that brings the principle to life. As you read, ask yourself,

- Does this story make sense to me?
- Do I remember a person like that?
- Do I remember such personal unselfishness, and did it work?
- How would my school look and feel if I were to adopt this behavior?

In each chapter, you will read some suggested intentional strategies for implementing these principles in your schools, and you'll meet some educators who have worked with the Eight Habits. I'll also offer some opportunities for you to participate—with some colleagues, I hope—in adapting these suggestions in your own school.

However, the Eight Habits of the Heart are more than mere concepts for intellectual discussion: They are people to become, actions to implement, commitments to live out, unselfishness to share, and daily tools to use in the process of building and sustaining community. It was the daily doings of the porch people that made the difference in the lives of their children. So powerful were their good acts that the full impact of legal segregation was aborted. The actions of our elders and our teachers brought civility out of rigid restrictions and a vision for our future out of a dimly lit past. Because of them, community replaced the chaos of racism and discrimination and provided the environment for the educational process.

We have access to these same principles today, and with them we too can defy the barriers and roadblocks to quality education and learning that we now face as we move into this new century, which holds great promise. With the principles the porch people practiced, you, too, over time will be able to build and sustain the communities you envision for your students.

Just as I needed this personal touch from the adults I encountered—caretakers, neighbors, and teachers—students still need it today. For many students in unfortunate personal circumstances, school may be the only place where they can be respected as individuals who have unlimited potential, the only place where great expectations of them exist. When this is the case, the educator becomes the practical and steady antidote to the troubled home environment, so please don't abdicate your role of personal involvement. I know it might be easy to teach by the book, but sometimes, you have to consider teaching by the heart.

Opportunity to Bring the
Human Touch to Your School

- Send a note to a student who needs encouragement.
- Take several students to lunch and make sure that the one who needs you is among those selected.
- Be patient with your students as you realize the internal burdens they carry.
- Whatever their progress, no matter how small and inconsistent, celebrate it with uttermost enthusiasm.

The future of our communities—of our nation and our world— depends on the young people who come to our schools every day. When we see young people as future trustees of our society, rather than as an aggregate of demographic data and social problems, we will naturally want to give them the best learning environment possible. As parents, caretakers (court-appointed guardians or foster parents), and especially as educators, you are uniquely positioned to provide it.

Building a great learning-teaching community is not a project but an ongoing process—one that must involve all heads, hands, and hearts! Working together happens best in an environment where people know each other and are committed to sustaining their relationships. Despite the daunting demands on today's educators, I still advocate that they carve out the time required to know each other. This one act alone will make a tremendous difference in the look and feel of your day.

Do you think we can replicate the collaborative unselfishness I found in Glen Allan for this generation of students? And if we set out to do this, what outcomes should we anticipate? When students and educators find themselves in such a community, both are positioned to achieve success. No machinery can duplicate that feeling.

Because of the efficiency, speed, and accuracy that are achievable with today's new technologies, we tend to underestimate the value of people and principles from another era. But we can't stand back and watch technology build community. Don't tie your hands behind your backs, and don't leave your heart in the parking lot.

Like your predecessors, you are called on to give your presence and your commitment, your unselfish acts, to rally students against low test scores, bad behavior, and underachievement. It may take a bit more time to include "the human touch" as part of your day, but it will be well worth it. In the midst of this technological revolution, we are challenged to invest ourselves in building community in the classroom, throughout the school, and on the playgrounds.

Within the communities defined by educators around the country, the convenience of the mouse and the mouse pad must not replace the much-needed touch—handshakes, heartfelt greetings, voices of expectation, shared conversations, and the much-needed thank-you notes. Continue to educate in a way that embraces community, even when you feel forced to meet requirements that focus on validating test scores, incorporating widespread technology, and matching the outcomes of scientific studies. If we have only this view of achievement as our total focus, how will we build an environment that will foster the success we all want?

There is reason for hope. As I said, I have witnessed firsthand the power of unselfishness to build community against all odds and have also over the years witnessed the outcomes of such efforts. The people of Glen Allan, Mississippi, living in the troubled final days of legal segregation, raised "the touch"—unselfish human involvement—to an art form. Their actions reveal the timeless and universal look and feel of what is needed to address the challenges and to take advantage of the opportunities within schools throughout America.

The students in your schools need this kind of caring environment to nurture their self-image and shape their dreams. I have met you at workshops and in schools and in university classrooms—you, the educators of today's America. I know you are up to the challenge of creating and sustaining this kind of community. These Eight Habits of the Heart will validate what many of you have always known—and have wished to experience: personal voice and personal touch as an essential part of the educational process. If by chance you have become weary or burned out due to troubled circumstances, I hope that seeing these timeless and universal habits lived out will serve as your personal guide to ensure your enthusiasm on behalf of our children, our students, and our future.

CHAPTER 4

Nurturing Attitude

The First Habit of the Heart

An Intentional Principle

*In our schools, a Nurturing
Attitude is characterized by unselfish caring,
supportiveness, and a willingness to share time.*

Simply put, a Nurturing Attitude is our way of saying that within this community, you can count on me to live beyond my personal needs because I care about others, and my life is strengthened and stretched as I reach into their lives. What better place than our schools to display such unselfishness? Embodied by a person, the Nurturing Attitude helps a new teacher maneuver through the tasks of satisfying all the local, state, and national demands made of educators. With students, the Nurturing Attitude shares a sandwich, offers a ride home, or shows up at a performance or a sports event where its presence wasn't required. The Nurturing Attitude visits a student's home just to tell the parents, "I enjoy teaching your child." And yes, the Nurturing Attitude continues that tradition of sharing quality time among all the adults who make up the educational team, not just the other teachers.

The Nurturing Attitude will not appear automatically. No matter how much we talk about it, write about it, or design posters to extol its virtues, we must also make an intentional commitment to the Nurturing Attitude if it is to truly become a reality. Other people and their concerns must become part of the force that drives our personal actions. After all, a Nurturing Attitude is unselfish caring—caring that reaches beyond our personal needs into the lives of others.

When embraced and lived out, a Nurturing Attitude will build and sustain a great learning-teaching community for our students and for the educators who are entrusted with their care. Keep in mind, this habit is not held captive by race, gender, or geography—it is freely available for your use as you educate, and it can help you to ensure a steady stream of productive citizens flowing from your school. Creating good citizens is a noble goal, one that will require consistent acts of unselfishness by educators on behalf of their students, by educators for each other, and among educators, students, and parents, binding them all in the school community.

This is what I encountered while growing up in the Mississippi Delta among the many porch people who meandered in and out of my life. And needless to say, this same level of unselfish caring found its way into our schools, embodied by school administrators, teachers, and staff who together saw their future through the lengthening steps of those of us who crossed their paths. Because they cared for us, they talked among themselves, shared what we today call "best practices," and most of all demonstrated an ongoing level of respect that we were able to witness. In so doing, we were left with the impression that all the adults at our school—the teachers, the bus drivers, the cooks, and the janitorial staff—were all one team working together on our behalf.

A similar picture is still needed, but embodying a Nurturing Attitude takes time and commitment. As a beneficiary of such unselfishness, however, I can validate that the return on any investment you make will be worth the cost. Focused unselfishness is needed to help us decide how to allocate our time. Although they may seem small, unselfish acts are indeed powerful; over time, such small acts will help build that steady stream of productive citizens we all wish to see.

Our 21st-century educational journey continues to provide opportunities to embody a Nurturing Attitude. Intentional support for your students and for those with whom you work, your voice of validation, your sharing of knowledge—all of these are still needed. Students today will see your good acts and how you manage the gift of time so that others might benefit. It just might catch on and show up among our students as they find reason to embrace this timeless principle.

A Nurturing Attitude is needed today more than ever as our lives are increasingly invaded by often depersonalizing technology and gadgets that allow us to go it alone and limit the conversations that are essential to building this habit of the heart. Successful education depends on getting to know each other, students and educators. Getting to know the people in our lives is the foundational requirement for a good community. It creates a place where great learning takes place.

But you can't get to know each other if everyone is dashing around trying to get a thousand things done. To focus on Nurturing Attitude, you'll be challenged to slow your pace. You can do this, so that you can really get to know your students and the colleagues who are part of your educational team. That's the first rule of building and sustaining community within your schools.

Like so many other things, I learned my first lessons about Nurturing Attitude from my great-grandfather, the Reverend Joe Young, known to me as Poppa Joe.

✒ From the Front Porch

I first saw this "slowing down" lived out by Poppa Joe, who could literally take 2½ hours to make a 28-mile trip in his 1949 Buick—and his speed had nothing to do with the car or the roads.

Of course, well before the trip started, I witnessed acts of unselfishness that were important to our day. First of all, Poppa had to lay aside his own personal Saturday morning agenda, which consisted of sitting on his front porch, soaking his feet in Epsom salts and water to get himself ready for another week of labor-intensive fieldwork. We were fieldworkers in that period of sharecropping and legal segregation, and both institutions could wear a person out. Poppa wasn't really being selfish in focusing on his health and his physical well-being.

Still, in the midst of his personal agenda, he took time to consider my request. I wanted to go to Greenville, Mississippi, to get frozen custard ice cream and hot French bread. No matter how odd this combination sounds, it really did taste good, and I considered it the ultimate treat. I still think about it today, and the memory brings smiles and a warmth I will always savor.

I badly needed someone to be there for me. I knew where I wanted to go. I wanted to go downtown to Washington Avenue to savor the smells from Brown's Bakery and to immediately go next door to the frozen custard stand, but I had no money for a bus and no car—anyway, I was much too young to drive. I needed others to be supportive of my needs, to be willing to share their time and let unselfish caring direct their efforts. I needed Poppa Joe. He was my only choice.

Poppa Joe accepted his leadership role. Somehow he knew that if he was to have an impact on the future, he had to deal with the present—and me—as inconvenient as it may have been for him. So he agreed to take me to Greenville.

Time after time, Poppa Joe and others in the little community of Glen Allan, Mississippi, put their needs to the side and did what was best for me. They left with me the notion that good deeds are more than a one-time commitment; they are instead consistent unselfishness lived out and passed along, what you might call a Nurturing Attitude. The same thing is true today. Everyone has a personal agenda, but sometimes it's a good idea to put that agenda on hold to help someone else—and not just once in a great while but every day. What would happen to your school community should students, parents, and educators adopt this type of commitment?

I was a beneficiary of my great-grandfather's unselfishness, an intangible quality added to the tangible gift of getting to Greenville. The long-term lesson was embodied in the journey itself—a journey that took hours when it could have ended in less than 40 minutes, while Poppa Joe showed me more of that Nurturing Attitude.

These situations are always coming up in life, the conflict of agendas, and the need for someone to make an unselfish decision.

- *Imagine that you are the only person who can provide the help someone else needs. What would you do?*

- *Would you rearrange your schedule to be the answer for a new teacher or a student who without you would not be able to move forward?*

- *If you're an administrator, will you deliberately and intentionally schedule time for classroom visits that aren't evaluative (to provide encouragement to students and teachers)?*

✏ From the Front Porch

Seated in the front seat of Poppa's car, my feet barely touched the floor, but I enjoyed the prestige of being at his side. I had someplace to go, but meantime, I was there for the ride—and what a ride it was, as I now reflect back. In the course of our trip, Poppa invited me into his world, where building relationships was a deliberate, everyday activity.

Instead of heading directly to the city, which would have been the sensible thing to do from my perspective, Poppa Joe drove that old Buick into the lives of our family and friends. He stopped and talked, shaking hands with nearly everyone seated on the front porches of our neighborhood and asking after their well-being. Poppa Joe's Nurturing Attitude covered everybody he knew.

Poppa made building relationships part of his daily routine. He slowed down and talked. If nobody was seated on the porch, he honked to make sure that no one was home before we moved on.

Poppa was determined to make a human contact. This is even more important today as communication devices seem to keep us connected, but not face-to-face, missing out on many important conversations. Maintaining eye contact must not become a lost art. A closed door or a face focused on a computer screen would not have stopped Poppa Joe from using that Nurturing Attitude to build community. It shouldn't stop you today. Be determined to make human contact while attending to your personal agenda.

Advanced technology will never replace face-to-face conversations. Building the community we define as ideal will always require that we carve out time for people. You won't be able to build alliances and collaborative teams without first having established relationships with the people around you. Establishing relationships needs to happen every day, as part of routine living; then, when a collective action is required, having these relationships already established pays off.

This is one lesson from the porch to consider: the value of your personal Nurturing Attitude in the lives of others—students, other educators, and the broader learning community. Your students need to witness this type of behavior—someday, it will also be required of them. I witnessed my great-grandfather building community, and today, it's my turn.

✨ From the Front Porch

At long last, we cleared all the houses in our small community, and just for a moment, I thought the road to Greenville was clear at last. Then, a new opportunity for Poppa Joe to display a Nurturing Attitude showed up, and my personal goals were delayed again. Our neighbor—we called him the hitchhiker—was standing in the road, smoking his pipe and ignoring Poppa's honking car horn.

I wanted Poppa to drive past him; after all, we had already spent more time with folks than I thought we should have. But Poppa stopped and picked up Mr. Louis Fields. I was devastated. I knew something was going to change. And it did. Poppa looked at me, and without his saying a word, I knew what I had to do. I had to leave the front seat where I was very comfortable and in control of the static-charged radio. And for a short period of time, I had to ride in the backseat as the two men talked back and forth—that was my contribution to Poppa's act of kindness. Before we went on to Greenville, my great-grandfather stopped to let Mr. Fields off at our small uptown area, where he would sit among his male friends, enjoying life and waving at those of us who passed by.

Many people are "standing in the middle of the road" at your school—the new teacher who needs your wealth of expertise, the new staff person who wants to be part of the educational team, and the students who need to know that they are at the top of your agenda, as well as the parents and caregivers who just might be intimidated by the sheer size of the school. To show a Nurturing Attitude, you have to slow down and stop—to provide your expertise and to validate your students' trust. Students who struggle to learn need the teacher to quietly pull them aside and provide that extra boost of encouragement. High achievers must not be left on their own to take care of themselves; they must be shown how to make the best use of their gifts.

> *Are you willing to give up the comfort of your "front seat"— perhaps your senior position in the school—to show your Nurturing Attitude and your willingness to take the time to build community?*
>
> *How can you use your position to build community?*
>
> *What actions can you take to ensure that you slow down to build relationships?*

There are many reasons you should stop and walk into the lives of members of the teaching-learning community at your school. A Nurturing Attitude will help focus your efforts. Like me, you may not want to stop because you're on your way someplace important or you're comfortable in the front seat. However, Poppa's vision included more than me, and I am glad it did. By stopping to pick up Mr. Fields, Poppa taught me that sharing the front seat—my perceived place of power—wouldn't keep me from accomplishing my objective in the long run. Though my great-grandfather stopped along the way to help others, he didn't lose sight of where we were headed. I got to where I wanted to go, and I was also taught to value helping others along the way. Both educators and students will benefit from such a ride, and so will the world in which we live.

I learned from Poppa's consistent unselfish acts that you cannot build an ideal teaching-learning community if you don't have time for *people.* As educators in today's society, you may well be living in schedule overload. Nevertheless, the youth in your care will still need time from you. You must figure a way to occasionally drop your agenda, crank up the old Buick, and head somewhere, just you and the youth in your care. No amount of gifts and gadgets will substitute for your time. My Poppa knew this!

As an educator, you may be bombarded with required new testing initiatives and new curriculums to implement, but one fact still remains true: Your students are at the core of your efforts, and getting to know them is still your best strategy for success. You might not need to slow down to design a new evaluation, but you must slow down if you are to build relationships with your students, their parents, and your peers.

I am definitely a beneficiary of such unselfishness and I suspect that many of you are as well. Poppa Joe wasn't the only resident of Glen Allan who showed me how to keep a Nurturing Attitude. I remember a teacher who included building relationships within the community as part of her lesson plan. In that long-ago time, society was riddled with difficulties, but not to the point that she felt it was acceptable to let the negativism of her environment dictate her actions.

You can probably guess that this was my first-grade teacher, Miss Mary Maxey—you met her in Chapter 1—a woman whose professional commitment reflected how she valued community. Although she juggled eight grades in one room, Miss Maxey still found time to visit parents and even to give some of us an important extracurricular encounter with the starlit night sky. Gathering some youngsters in a clearing near the school, Miss Maxey told us that we were just like those stars—bright, gifted, and shining—even in the daylight when you couldn't see them. The stars were always shining, she said, and she expected no less from us. I was a beneficiary of someone who allowed unselfish vision to determine how her time would be used.

Remember, in my small community, the porch people were known for engaging in conversations from which incredible possibilities emerged. They deliberately placed themselves in the path of others. In your daily rounds, don't make a quick turn to avoid a conversation, but walk briskly into the opportunity. This is what community is all about. The porch people had no idea that their lives would one day become a model for others; they were moved to unselfishness by their own hearts and personal observations. I believe the same will happen for you as you talk with others about slowing the pace and taking the time to build community by deliberately focusing on people, their needs, and your opportunity to embody a Nurturing Attitude.

Intentional Strategies for Promoting a Nurturing Attitude

In our schools, a Nurturing Attitude is characterized by unselfish caring, supportiveness, and a willingness to share time.

- Take time to learn each student's name, and always use students' names when engaging them in lessons.
- Learn at least one personal interest or goal for each of your students. At least once a week, talk to each student about this interest or goal, as well as about the student's academic performance. Support your students' endeavors. (Why not attend their athletic events, concerts, or plays? Be there!)
- Get to know students better by visiting their homes—then stop to say hello whenever you meet their parents in the community.
- Invite parents into the school to work with students or help with homework.
- Visit the cafeteria once a week and sit with different students each time. Have lunch with a different student every day.
- Create activities for students away from the school environment in which you can share their concerns and interests.

(Continued)

- Collaborate with fellow teachers to do group lesson plans and projects.
- Show your concern for the community by getting your students involved—with you, of course—in extracurricular service projects (visiting elderly, visiting sick children).
- Write thank-you notes, and send a newsletter to parents. Share thoughts, quotes, and inspirational sayings with others on a regular basis.

These strategies for using the timeless and universal tool of Nurturing Attitude to build community within classrooms and schools were developed by other educators. Stop and think of several additional strategies that you'd like to see added to this list, strategies that speak specifically to your school's objectives for excellence.

Opportunity to Promote a Nurturing Attitude in Your School

Ask your fellow educators to brainstorm with you about how you can bring this life lesson into your school.

- How can you make time to speak to each student so that you're sure everyone understands the lesson?
- How can you find time for getting to know your students, their parents, and your peers?
- How can you turn the teacher's lounge into a 21st-century front porch, a place where reflective conversations take place and great possibilities emerge?

Educators Just Like You . . . and Nurturing Attitude

I've seen the Nurturing Attitude embodied by educators in all parts of the world. For example, I visited the wintry cold of northern Minnesota for the first time at the request of an elementary school principal, Kevin Kopperud. He decided to support others by working with his district to communicate the concepts of community I had described at a national conference in San Antonio, Texas. As Kevin said,

> The ideas in the book helped build a foundation for us to think more intentionally about community in our schools and what we could do to promote stronger community. As a result, book groups were formed in our school district to read and study *Eight Habits*. . . . His stories from the Delta and ideas about community moved hundreds of people from our schools and city to become involved in building a stronger sense of community.

Closer to home in Columbus, Georgia, Lura Reed, the principal of Dimon Elementary School, implemented what she had learned about Nurturing Attitude when I spoke as a guest professor at Harvard University's Principals' Center. My concept of building a powerful school community resonated with her, and she invited me to come to her school and talk about these timeless principles with her staff as part of a required professional development workshop.

I'll always remember how I felt upon entering her building. The Nurturing Attitude was alive there—unselfish caring, being supportive of others, and being willing to share your time. I saw it first as I entered the school with all "my stuff," not quite knowing which way to go. The custodian held the door open for me and smiled as if the school was her very own. The mutual respect between principal and custodian would become evident, and I would leave their school with an updated picture of what happens when both treasure their respective positions.

Thoughts of Mr. Powell, the janitor in Glen Allan when I was an elementary student, flooded my mind as I took special notice of how the students respectfully responded to the custodian and how she proudly responded to them as if she was indeed the educator—and in some sense she really was. I followed her as she gave of her time, leading me to the library where my host and her teachers were waiting, instead of just pointing the way.

Ms. Reed told me how she used the Nurturing Attitude to lay the groundwork so that all Eight Habits would be part of her school:

> As a Principal, it was important to me that each faculty/staff member see themselves as one or each of these "Habits," because as role models we could instill these "Habits" into our children. . . . It is our belief at Dimon that accountability is not just ascribed to test scores, but to the education of the whole child. In an effort to build community, one child at a time, we as teachers must truly possess and model these habits for our children.

As a component of integrating *Eight Habits of the Heart,* each grade level is asked to share the following information at assigned faculty meetings.

1. What did you do to promote, encourage, model, and teach to children the Habit of the Month?

2. Discuss or share how the habit applies to each of you as a grade level or group.

3. Who do you believe exemplifies the Habit of the Month and why?

The grade levels submit the names of two students and one faculty or staff member for recognition as best displaying the Habit of the Month. Their pictures are placed in the hallway on the Habit Tree, and they are honored at a schoolwide assembly at the conclusion of the school year.

You might adapt this Dimon Elementary School activity for use at your school.

CHAPTER 5

Responsibility

The Second Habit of the Heart

An Intentional Principle

In our schools, Responsibility is showing and encouraging a personal commitment to each task.

Once we have slowed our lives enough to nurture, we are more likely to be there to help in the development of others by sharing our knowledge and skills. When we unselfishly focus on how we use our time, we are more likely to make a personal commitment to the various tasks that we all might be facing. In such situations, we allow others to learn from us as we embrace their gifts, which, over time, create shared skill sets. Responsibility comes alive in such an environment, not just for adults but for students as well.

First of all, Responsibility knows how to do something for the benefit of others and do it well. Being responsible is not the same as being skilled, however. Responsibility requires that someone shows up—it's all about commitment and consistency. Responsibility is a consistent contributor, even when contributing may be personally inconvenient. Responsibility understands that we are all linked in a community, and almost anything we do—or don't do—may have consequences far beyond what we ourselves will feel, or even see. Responsibility pays serious attention to ensuring that those consequences are as good as possible and that negative outcomes are minimized.

Responsibility is an unselfish person, a person who has embraced knowledge and skills for a greater purpose and derives great joy from his or her efforts. Over the years, hundreds of educators and their professional peers have told me that without this habit of the heart, their work would not get done. Responsibility shows up in the people we encounter and their willingness to share their knowledge and demonstrate their skills, and usually, they are responsible because someone else unselfishly showed them how it was done. This is community. Responsibility is an essential part of its structure.

In my hometown, Cleve Mormon, our iceman, was the embodiment of Responsibility: a commitment to tasks and getting things done. Giving his full attention to each chore, he was both hands-on and "heart-on" in everything he did, including training me to be his assistant. His ongoing efforts to teach me his trade were more effective than any onetime meeting or quick e-mail could ever have been.

Mr. Cleve "showed up," a southern term that means he was physically and emotionally present for me when I was just a young boy. Forty years later, I am still reaping the benefits of his unselfish investment in me.

✌ From the Front Porch

By the time I became a bona fide teenager, I was tired of picking cotton. I wanted a man-type job, and I had my eye on one job in particular: working at Mr. Cleve's icehouse. I had watched other young men work for him over the years, and I felt that it was now my turn. I had no experience to offer, however; this job required skills beyond my capabilities.

Mr. Cleve was one of the best small-business owners in our community. Would I be able to make the leap from the fields to his business? To get there, I needed someone who was generous with his time and unselfish about sharing knowledge. If I was to succeed, Mr. Cleve had to allow me to observe and adopt his skills, knowledge, and perspectives. And that's how I spent my time after school and on Saturdays, just watching Mr. Cleve work.

He wasn't much of a talker, but what a lesson in Responsibility he taught! He not only understood the job inside and out, he had the knowledge and the respect of those he served. The local cotton planters, the general stores, and the truckloads of fieldworkers who were his customers could do their jobs better because of his commitment to every little detail required to be successful in the ice business. This is what I observed, as well as the excitement and joy on his face at the end of the day. Being responsible does indeed bring its own rewards.

Mr. Cleve was well aware how important his commitment and consistency were, and he knew what he had to do to ensure those outcomes. He also knew that I had to understand and embrace the notion that the required commitment would result from a process of hands-on involvement and mental acceptance.

At first I did little odd jobs at the icehouse; then slowly, he began to let me handle tasks associated with actually cutting and selling ice. I stood and watched a lot. I needed more than a one-hour crash course in icehouse management to embody the look and feel of a person committed to the task. At the end of the training, my actions had to show enough assurance and confidence that Mr. Cleve would feel comfortable leaving me in charge.

To be good trustees of our society, students will need Responsibility, and educators can share knowledge that helps build a foundation for this habit of the heart. However, Responsibility is best shared when we as adults fully embrace its importance. As you do your job, keep in mind that you are always having an impact on your students: They are more likely to do what they see you do.

- *When you started working at your school, did you feel as eager but inexperienced as I felt with Mr. Cleve?*

- *Now that you have some experience, can you "be Mr. Cleve" for new teachers or staff in your school?*

- *How could you allow them to tap into your wealth of experience as they become part of your teaching-learning community?*

What better place than among your peers to demonstrate and exhibit Responsibility in tangible ways? Your unselfish actions toward your peers will define the look and feel of Responsibility in your life. As this habit becomes commonplace among all who are part of the educational process, students will benefit from your natural way of being.

In building good community, you are never far removed from the opportunity to build up others, and no one knows this better than educators. Opportunity is right across from your desk, running down the halls, playing on the playgrounds, and yes, even sitting across from you in the teachers' lounge or lunchroom or in the classroom down the hall.

You'll recall that Mr. Cleve responded to my need to know by first giving me tasks that I could accomplish. In so doing, he built up my confidence. As confidence was built, excuses and fear subsided. He allowed me to observe his actions, thereby providing the model of excellence I would need. As a result of his personal involvement and his sharing of knowledge, I was soon able to graduate from small tasks to the much bigger tasks associated with running an icehouse.

🐚 From the Front Porch

The icehouse was a busy place in 1958, and it was particularly exciting in the morning as scores of field trucks loaded with workers—many of them pretty girls just my age and maybe a little older from the city—drove into Glen Allan for day work. Because the Mississippi Delta is known for its intense heat, their workday could not begin without a stop at the only icehouse in town.

I wanted to be in the middle of the action, but this was more easily said than done. Mr. Cleve was the source for my learning, and the icehouse was a beehive of activity. In spite of the many demands on his attention, he nevertheless took the time to talk to me and, when there was a lull, to show me how to cut 300-pound blocks of ice into the appropriate sizes. He also demonstrated how to count money, give change, and how to treat the customers. He made sure that I understood what was required of me, and he showed me through example how to meet those requirements.

His desire to see me succeed drove his consistency. I am so glad he cared. I had many questions, and he was there with ready answers, providing me what I needed at the moment and later adding to the knowledge, until before long I was able to demonstrate skills I never thought I'd have. In the end, his sense of commitment and consistency became my very own.

In a community, questions are an essential part of the conversation, and so are answers. As Mr. Cleve involved himself in the hands-on teaching process, I became Responsibility by becoming committed to the tasks; besides learning how to cut and sell ice, I learned the Responsibility that was essential for my personal success as well as the success of his business. Because I was the beneficiary of Mr. Cleve's unselfishness, hundreds of others whom I waited on at the icehouse became the beneficiaries of my attitude and my skills.

> • *Can you become Mr. Cleve for the benefit of your students?*
> • *If you do, what will this mean for your students?*

The young people and the adults who see you model Responsibility will share my good fortune. I encourage you to weather the storms that attempt to steer you away from the students and fellow educators who need you. Responsibility and the personal commitment that drives it are compatible not only with test-result mandates but also with our more profound educational goals.

We all agree that the principle of Responsibility is an important and necessary piece of our values and ideals, but like a Nurturing Attitude, it will not show up in your school unless one person brings it in and another provides a warm welcome. What have you learned from the story of the iceman?

Intentional Strategies for Promoting Responsibility

In our schools, Responsibility is showing and encouraging a personal commitment to each task.

- Enforce established rules that students are to follow.
- Don't *tell* others what to do; *show* them.
- Arrive at work at the established time.
- Turn in lesson plans on time.
- Hold students accountable for meeting established deadlines.
- Involve parents in creating a positive learning and working environment.

(Continued)

- Teach the students more than they expect to learn.
- Send a motivational or inspirational note to students' homes every month.

These strategies for using the timeless and universal tool of Responsibility to build community within classrooms and schools were developed by other educators. Stop and think of several additional strategies that you'd like to see added to this list, strategies that speak specifically to your school's objectives for excellence.

Opportunity to Promote Responsibility in Your School

Setting goals with students and keeping an eye on how they measure up will help students develop Responsibility.

- Have students write down their goals.
- Check to see if those goals have been reached at the beginning of each quarter.
- If students have reached their goals, encourage them to set higher standards next time.
- If not, help them figure out why they didn't reach their goals, and help them develop a strategy to move forward.

Educators Just Like You . . . and Responsibility

When I think of Responsibility, I think of Rigdon Road Elementary School in Columbus, Georgia, where Mrs. Phyllis Jones is the principal.

I met Principal Jones through Lura Reed, whose work at Dimon Elementary was described in Chapter 4. On the very first day I spent at Rigdon Road School with Mrs. Jones and her educators, I experienced the dynamics of commitment and consistency that define Responsibility embraced and lived out.

Becoming this habit of the heart empowers individuals, and these teachers all seemed empowered. They knew what was going on, and they were going about their many tasks with confidence and pride. What I saw on Rigdon Road was much the same as what I had experienced so long ago at the icehouse in Glen Allan, Mississippi, where Mr. Cleve's shared commitment and consistency empowered me.

In Columbus, Georgia, Mrs. Jones was the team builder, with Responsibility at the core of her efforts. This principal covered all her bases, and she was excited about her work and about her people, all of them. In a recent conversation, she told me that she and two of her teachers, Mrs. Pamela Thompson and Mrs. Berderia Fuller, along with Mrs. Smithie Vaughn, a parent, had become immersed in the Cornerstone Literacy Project, which ensures that students get every opportunity for reading success. The four of them became "Mr. Cleve" for the school's teachers and parents. The complete process of model and critique was in place, and so were the commitment and consistency that were needed to empower them all.

The more people who embody Responsibility, the better for the students who will be the beneficiaries. According to Mrs. Jones, "What separates Rigdon Road Elementary School from any other ordinary school in the community is its collective sense of commitment to guiding principles that articulate what the people in the school believe and what they seek to create." Just like Mr. Cleve, the educators and parents at Rigdon Road are committed and up to the task.

When Responsibility becomes part of your educational strategy, it helps turn your thoughtful plans into reality. It gives you the patience and the excitement you need to bring others to the process.

CHAPTER 6

Dependability

The Third Habit of the Heart

An Intentional Principle

*In our schools, Dependability is being there
for others through all the time of their lives, a
steady influence that makes tomorrow a welcome event.*

Dependability is essential for building your ideal learning-teaching community, and it does not stand alone. It builds on both Nurturing Attitude and Responsibility. Dependability is more than a mere word or a habit that we often chide coworkers and students for not having. Dependability is a person. It looks like educators all over the world who are committed to the success of their students. If an educator or student refuses to *become* this habit, then the teaching-learning community we desire will not show up.

To become this habit of the heart is to understand the importance of your word, your commitment to others. Over time, how you live out your word becomes the definition of who you are. Of course, this habit works best when we all understand and embrace its importance, when we become a team that is well coordinated and committed to everyone's success. However, when the ideal is not present in the community, it becomes even more important for those who recognize its value to stand firm in their right acts. Your peers will see this, as will the students in your school. For many students, and even for some of the adults with whom you work, you may be the only expression of this timeless and universal principle that they are privileged to see.

For me, Dependability will always be embodied in the person who stood on her front porch, even on cold mornings, to alert our bus driver that I was indeed going to school. It was my great-aunt, Mama Ponk. She became this habit of the heart, and I was the beneficiary of her unselfishness. In my uncertain world of legal segregation, Dependability had to be more than promising words or even an entire conversation expressing concern. It had to be a lived commitment. In those difficult times, I personally needed someone who was ready to commit.

ᴂ From the Front Porch

Because of legal segregation, I had to travel nearly 100 miles round-trip each day to our county seat in order to attend high school. I had to do this for four years, and I was successful. I graduated from Norma C. O'Bannon High School with perfect attendance; I was valedictorian of my graduating class. The crisis was the journey: getting to school each day, even though it was miles from my home. I was able to accomplish my goal because my great-aunt, Mama Ponk, who was raising me at the time, voluntarily became Dependability.

Mama Ponk made a plan of action. First, she entered into a dialogue with our bus driver, Mr. Murray, and made sure that he was going to show up. You see, if I missed that bus, there was no other bus, and no one available to drive me to the city. I had to catch the one and only bus that came by our house. Second, Mama Ponk made sure that I understood that I had to get up. And last, she stated her role in the process.

Mama Ponk committed herself to being on the front porch every school day to pull the cord that turned the front porch light on and off—the signal to the driver that he had business at our house. Her unselfishness in dedicating herself to that task alerted Mr. Murray as his bus turned the corner that I was going to school. She did this day in and day out during the dark winter months, standing on the porch in a flannel gown, her head tightly wrapped in a scarf, when the early mornings were as dark as night.

More than a conversation was needed to make this happen. My great-aunt could have easily said, "Baby, I talked with the driver, now you get up and see if you can make it." Instead, she became part of the process, and what she did ensured that I would know how to exhibit this habit in my life.

To be fully realized, Dependability requires not only a well-thought-out plan but also someone's commitment to the personal action required on his or her part to make that plan work. It is not enough to observe what is needed or to be able to articulate what is missing. Dependability requires action. Pulling a light cord may be a simple action, but the consistency of the effort changed my life. Dependability as a fully engaged habit is developed over time through multiple microdosages of unselfish acts.

Of course, it takes time to create programs and plans, and the finished product may be quite impressive. Sometimes, we become so impressed with our plans and programs that we fail to insert ourselves into the mix as the "active yeast" that turns the plans into real change. Mama Ponk factored herself into the equation that set me on the road to achievement. Dependability requires the commitment of being personally involved, no matter who benefits.

How can you become Mama Ponk for your class?

How can you become part of the answer for a problem you have observed?

How will you determine the level of your involvement?

If you became Mama Ponk, what could this type of commitment mean to a new teacher, a fellow employee, or a new or shy student?

My great-aunt made the commitment and became Dependability. She was there for me in words and deeds. She became the active yeast in our plan. I would not have been able to do all that was required each morning had she not volunteered to be there for me. In fact, without her involvement on a consistent basis, I am not sure if I'd be writing this book today. The positive outcomes happened for me because of the "human touch" she lived out.

Your ideal learning-teaching community will benefit from the same level of touch as I experienced. Should Dependability infuse your school, trust and follow-through may become commonplace. Our schools and our lives are better lived in the presence of Dependability. Dependability distilled into specific recommendations will take on many different looks based on your school.

Underlying Dependability is the idea that being there for others is important and necessary. This concept has been verified not only by the porch people of the Mississippi Delta but also by Rob Lebow in his highly successful 1990 book, *The Journey into the Heroic Environment:*

Imagine a place where everyone puts the interests of others before their own. Where everyone tells the truth and where trust and mentoring abound. That place is called a Heroic Environment.

As part of his research, he reviewed thousands of tests given to employees in many types of organizations over a long period of time and found eight values that people most often seek. He called these "people values." One of those values—putting the interest of others above your own—is actually a look into the heart of Dependability. If you put the interests of your students and your peers on the front burner in your daily life, you will actualize this habit of Dependability within your school.

The theme of this chapter—and this book—is personal unselfishness: educators standing up and reaching out. Unselfishness cannot be e-mailed, nor can Dependability. Dependability, as we have seen it expressed in Mama Ponk's story, is required to balance the technology-related depersonalization that is creeping into our schools. We still need to experience the dynamics that come only from the personal interactions of students, teachers, and other educators, educators who have that "human touch."

Keep in mind that you are educating the trustees of your community's future.

Your students must encounter Dependability if they are to know how it looks and feels, to value its importance. Our students still need someone willing to stand on the front porch and make sure the bus stops . . . on their behalf. How can you flip on the light for the students in your school and the educators with whom you serve?

Intentional Strategies to Promote Dependability

In our schools, Dependability is being there for others through all the time of their lives, a steady influence that makes tomorrow a welcome event.

- Designate a day each week to take students to a particular activity, and then do it consistently.
- Never go into a classroom underprepared.
- Return graded papers when you promised.

(Continued)

(Continued)

- If a student is absent two days in a row, contact his or her home.
- Be consistent in your educational approach and your work habits, so students learn what to expect from you.
- Be consistent in your respect for your students, so they can feel confident of your regard for them.
- Consider being at school 45 minutes early and staying 30 minutes after classes end so that you can talk with students or help another teacher.
- Smile first thing and welcome students to school every morning—let them know you're glad to see them, whether you are in a good mood or not. Start the day positively.
- Devise a follow-up calendar and a reminder calendar.
- Devote time and energy to learning effective teaching strategies so that when the students arrive they will be given opportunities to enjoy learning.

These strategies for using the timeless and universal tool of Dependability to build community within classrooms and schools were developed by other educators. Stop and think of several additional strategies that you'd like to see added to this list, strategies that speak specifically to your school's objectives for excellence.

Opportunity to Promote Dependability in Your School

Form a group of teachers, and map out a strategy to use successful students to work across classes, where appropriate, to bolster the work habits and the outcomes of students who are not doing so well.

(Continued)

If you're a coach, remind your athletes that they are a team and depend on each other. If they are to achieve the group's goals, then everyone must do his or her part. If anyone becomes undependable, the team falters.

Adapt the coaching strategy in your classroom and school. Set a group goal, and engage the team in achieving it.

Put in a place a system to ensure that school administrators are available to all stakeholders and that requests from teachers, students, parents, and members of the community get prompt replies.

Educators Just Like You . . . and Dependability

I met Kennedy Dixon at a conference in California and later spoke in Long Beach, where he was a middle-school educator. As a southerner brought up in Georgiana, Alabama—a community much like Glen Allan, Mississippi—Mr. Dixon recognized the porch people from his own youth, but he also saw that the timeless values they represented could be used anywhere.

Mr. Dixon had an opportunity to be there for one of his best teachers, a curriculum coach at a middle school, who asked for his help dealing with the most challenging class of her career, a group of students who had failed reading several times and seemed to lack any motivation to learn. Mr. Dixon introduced her to my books, both *Once Upon a Time When We Were Colored* and *Eight Habits of the Heart,* and together, they developed a curriculum around those values. Dependability is a person, a person committed to the success of others, and that describes Mr. Dixon. Here's his story:

> The class viewed the movie, *Once Upon A Time When We Were Colored* and began reading *Eight Habits of the Heart.* . . . I would often visit the class and model lessons. . . .

After a few months, the students' attitude began to change regarding their classroom and overall academics. During various reading activities, they would identify several characters that exemplified each of the habits. Using a myriad of teaching strategies while continuing to focus on *Eight Habits of the Heart* and community building, [the teacher's] classroom transformed into a true community.

Later, data from this class were compared with data from classes that had not received the community building strategies, and students using the new curriculum outperformed their peers; the coach's reading class was the only reading class in which *every* student passed and met the benchmark for his or her work.

Long Beach is not the Delta, but the concepts Mr. Dixon and his curriculum coach embraced proved that the Eight Habits are powerful and transformational strategies anywhere. It took more than Mr. Dixon's Dependability; it took his personal commitment to bring about the change that was needed, and his teacher also was there for her students. Together, they created a community in which everyone thrived.

CHAPTER 7

Friendship

The Fourth Habit of the Heart

An Intentional Principle

*In our schools, Friendship is the habit that binds
people together when we take pleasure in each other's
company, listen, laugh, and share good times and bad.*

Y our ideal learning-teaching community will not come into existence without the presence of Friendship, the habit that binds people together because of established positive relationships. Friendship stands at the door to welcome students and extends warm invitations to parents and others who care about the children. Friendship knows the bus driver and talks regularly with the cooks. Friendship welcomes the cleaning crew, and students are shown the look and feel of offering respect. Friendship writes notes of encouragement to students and sometimes sends thank-you notes to parents. Friendship talks with other educators to ensure that a troubled student has been assessed properly and that everyone in the school is weaving a net of protection and expectation on the student's behalf.

For your students, Friendship is more than a high-five or a nod of the head. It is not enough for educators to wish that *students* will develop this habit; educators must personally embrace friendships among their peers and with the parents of the students who attend their school.

In our building community workshops, we often challenge our participant educators to take a signed check of five figures or more and travel with me—in their imagination, of course—to a major discount store where some version of everything we need is in stock. I then ask them to walk up and down the aisles to find me at least one gallon of Friendship. Of course, everyone laughs, and for a brief moment, the educators face the reality that Friendship—although it's worth quite a bit more than even a five-figure check—cannot be purchased and dispensed at will.

As an educator, you need to experience this habit of the heart, and human beings can practice this habit only with another human being. Friendship exists from our personal efforts to give it life. When you become this habit by your deliberate acts of unselfishness in your classrooms, teachers' lounges, schools, and homes, you encourage "the human touch," the same unselfish personal acts that are essential to give life to your ideal learning-teaching community.

My great-aunt, Mama Ponk, personalized Dependability during my time in high school, a gift that was so critical to my graduation. Dependability stopped the bus, but it was the habit of Friendship that sustained me while I was on the bus and when a shy country student found himself in school with guys and girls from the city.

✌ From the Front Porch

After nearly 40 years, I still remember my high school friends, those who stepped up and welcomed me, Frank Johnson, Billy Perry and Henderson Fields, Mary Lou Anderson, Emma Bradley, and others who overlooked my upbringing and celebrated our common humanity.

I was unable to dress as well as many students—even some of my friends. I had little or no extra money, so I was unable to do those extra high school-type things. These two things alone could have hampered my relationships and negatively impacted my learning. But the Friendship I needed showed up in the persons of the students I've named here.

Once friendships were established, my lack of proper dress became a nonissue, and my lack of money to compete with them gave my friends an opportunity to share with me. And, you know, those youthful acts of unselfishness that I encountered still impact me today and challenge me to do likewise.

"Jump in the car, man." In high school, those words are music to your ears, and when the popular students overlook your lack of fashionable dress and welcome you to the best years of your life, community is definitely being formed, and Friendship is leading the way. Dressed in starched khakis and equally starched button-down-collar shirts, Frank, Billy, and Sammie Hudson would race for the parking lot as soon as the noon bell sounded. Frank had his own car, and it was parked there.

The three had a routine, one I wanted to be part of, but I looked so different from them in dress and in grooming style. They went to the fashionable black barbershops on Nelson Street in downtown Greenville, while I still had my hair cut by Mr. Will, who worked off his back porch in Glen Allan, where community gossip was more important than learning a new style.

The first time I attempted to join in, I ran toward the parking lot, but on a path that would let me change course if I wasn't invited. Then, I heard the magic words: "Hey, man, jump in the car."

I needed Friendship then, and students still need such environments today; thus, educators need to strategically focus on making this principle a real part of their schools. Friendship is a powerful habit when practiced in the presence of others. Start by letting your students see the friendships you have with your colleagues. Genuine Friendship is more than embracing professional courtesy. Genuine Friendship is getting to know the educators with whom you work and making time in your day to nurture those relationships. This habit of the heart is too valuable to the school community to leave unattended. In the broadest sense of the word, Friendship extends the vision of both parties, the giver and the receiver.

> *How can you use Friendship to make all students feel included?*
>
> *What happens to the student who feels like an outsider in class?*
>
> *Do you feel that positive relationships can impact learning?*

Although I enjoyed my new friends in high school, life would not have been complete had not several of the teachers also "become" this habit on my behalf. Take, for example, Mrs. Millicent Jackson, my high school science teacher—we called her Miss Jackson, in the southern style.

From the Front Porch

Miss Jackson's Friendship validated all the others. As an adult with position and influence, she both welcomed us and showed others the value of doing so. Her unselfishness made the difference in my learning process, not just in *her* class, but in my other classes as well. Because of her view of us and how she treated us, her country cousins who had come to town to be educated, Friendship flourished.

From Miss Jackson's perspective, we were bright young men and women with tremendous capacity. We didn't dress as well as our city counterparts, nor did we speak as well, but that reality did not shape Miss Jackson's view of us. Maybe my science teacher saw our potential and responded accordingly. Maybe, just maybe, she saw future trustees of our community.

We were from the country, but Miss Jackson ignored all the telltale signs. Just as if we were city kids, she called us by our last names, not our first names or the pet names we had heard all our lives. We were given the chance to participate in major projects. And most of all, we were invited to her city home.

Miss Jackson lived on Delta Street in Greenville, Mississippi, in a large rambling ranch-style house, bigger than any house I had ever seen and definitely larger than any house owned by African Americans in my small cotton community. I was shy. However, Miss Jackson welcomed me to the party and invited me to taste my first finger food. I was also introduced to her beautiful high school-age daughter, and after a period of time and measured quietness, I opened up and began to laugh and talk with the others.

It wasn't easy. They had memories from the city and Saturday nights on Nelson Street, and all of my memories were from the country, in the same county and state, but worlds apart. Miss Jackson, however, embraced our shared humanity and potential. Today, I do the same for others if I feel that my voice of welcome and my embrace of Friendship can make a difference.

Miss Jackson befriended us, and our educational process was the beneficiary of her unselfish acts. In my case, both teachers and my fellow students had gifts to share, and Friendship provided the place for it to happen. Without their Friendship, I have no doubt that my high school experience could have turned out disastrous. It's important to keep in mind that good relationships promote good learning. If a student feels left out and cast aside, focusing on subjects takes the backseat or no seat at all.

> *How will you exemplify Friendship among your peers?*
>
> *How would your day look if there were no Friendship in your life?*
>
> *What will the presence of Friendship ensure within your school?*

When it is lived out in the presence of others, Friendship becomes contagious. Because Miss Jackson welcomed us to the school and treated us with respect, the students and even other teachers were challenged to create a welcoming environment for all of us. Miss Jackson's actions set the stage for the positive acts of others, and all of these were necessary for us to maximize our potential as high school students.

You can have the same impact today. It is within your power to show others the value of this habit of the heart. Anticipation and vision are key components of ensuring sensory contact in all the places of our lives, not just on school campuses or in the Mississippi Delta nearly a half century ago. As you set out to become Friendship in your school, your students and your fellow educators will find themselves benefiting from your anticipation of their needs. When we anticipate the needs of others and provide that assistance, we extend their vision. And this is what we want for our young students—the future trustees of our communities. We want to expand their vision of themselves and the world in which they live. As an educator, you play a critical role in this process.

Even before I went to high school, I knew that the actions of adults could make the difference. I had seen it within my home, and of course,

I experienced it from Miss Maxey, our first-grade teacher. Some people might suppose that she reached out to us because she was one of us. She came from our community. What about the educator who was not from such a small rural environment? Would he or she have the wherewithal to make an unselfish difference?

✨ From the Front Porch

I know a teacher who used her gifts of travel and experience, not to put us down but to build us up. Miss Johnnie Mae Harris, a teacher from the city, found time and ways to expand our vision of ourselves. She made us feel that being at our small school with us was the height of her career. She never looked down on us. She became an inspiration, someone to emulate. She knew our names. She respected our parents. She talked with us and, in so doing, was able to learn our dreams.

And in her gracious way, she found ways to ensure us that we could extend our borders beyond Glen Allan, Mississippi. Rather than just dwell on subject material that was common to our neighborhood, she brought the vast knowledge of the world to us and made us feel part of all that was going on. And you know, I remember that she dressed up for us! Even if the contract required that she do so, she lifted us to a higher level of thinking and, yes, grooming. Through her class, we were given a window into a world that let us stretch our imagination.

Miss Harris's excitement became ours, and in her fourth-grade class, we achieved beyond expectations. She never lowered the bar. She taught us how to rise to the bar. She introduced us to prose and poetry—long poems that seem to have no end—and she helped us learn to write great papers. She anticipated the arrival of students she viewed as first class and, in so doing, planned her lessons to extract the best that we had to offer.

In our schools, students are surrounded by many hands and many hearts. If these hands and hearts fully understand their role, they will respond to the needs of their students as the community of Glen Allan responded to me. At the school where Miss Harris was a teacher, the principal led the way in making our learning experience caring and welcoming. Friendship was modeled from the top. We can do this today and leave 21st-century examples of how such a habit can look and feel. Friendship must not be taken for granted. It will not show up in your school unless you, your peers, and your students bring it.

How can this habit look in your school? What could you commit to doing each and every day to ensure that your school becomes a 21st-century caring environment? How can you make your school a place where Friendship thrives?

Intentional Strategies to Promote Friendship

In our schools, Friendship is the habit that binds people together when we take pleasure in each other's company, listen, laugh, and share good times and bad.

- Consider home visits as an opportunity to extend this habit of the heart.
- Be open and display a positive attitude.
- Listen to what the students have to say and extend support in the appropriate manner.
- Extend invitations to parents to become actively involved.
- Consider giving an extra day on assignments to those students who may be at home alone with no one to make them study.

(Continued)

- Help students create a community of Friendship in school by finding that special talent each child might contribute to the community.
- Change seating arrangements or learning group partners to encourage classroom friendships through common goals.
- Write one thank-you note every week, either to an adult or a student who has listened, laughed, or shared an experience. Once a month, write a note to someone inviting that person to share a memory with your class.

These strategies for using the timeless and universal tool of Friendship to build community within classrooms and schools were developed by other educators. Stop and think of several additional strategies that you'd like to see added to this list, strategies that speak specifically to your school's objectives for excellence.

Opportunity to Promote Friendship in Your School

Form class exchanges by having teachers and students from some classes as guests in other classes. In this way, you show the connectivity of the educational process and, most important, establish reasons to work and study together.

Talk to your students about local and world events, what's happening in the community or school—get to know your students, their worries, their accomplishments, their interests. And share your hobbies and interests with them, so they see you as "more of a real person."

Educators Just Like You . . . and Friendship

I call it Friendship, but it could also be called the Fourth R. That's what Kennedy Dixon—whom you met in the previous chapter—calls it. I'll let him tell you about how he learned the Fourth R back home in Georgiana, Alabama, at an elementary school much like mine:

> We had always heard how important it was for schools to give you the "three R's" referring to reading, writing, and arithmetic. However, as I fondly recall the classrooms at Austin Elementary School, I am constantly reminded that I was given the much-needed Fourth R, which stands for *Relationship*. Each of us had our own personal relationship with all of our teachers during elementary and middle school.

Perhaps the most influential of Mr. Dixon's school friendships was with Mr. Abrams, a former teacher who is now principal of Robert L. Austin Elementary School. They visited when Mr. Dixon made a recent trip home:

> As always, we walked the halls of the school and discussed our lives, past, present, and future plans. As he did when I was growing up, he offered encouragement, kind words and laughter, no matter what topic we discussed.
>
> Over the years, Mr. Abrams and I had become good friends. I often called him when perplexed with issues, both personal and professional. We often converse over the phone for hours at a time as he continues to provide me with unconditional guidance and support.
>
> While discussing issues teachers face in guiding today's students, he stated, "You can't teach them, if you can't reach them."

I once had the opportunity to see that Mr. Dixon was applying this valuable lesson from his former teacher. He had invited me to share the stories of my Mississippi childhood with a group of California students who had been defined as at-risk. Some were teenage mothers and fathers, and all faced a variety of social challenges.

How can you model acceptance for youth who have been defined as at-risk?

What can you bring into their daily lives to give them a different picture of themselves and their circumstances?

As we arrived at the school, I was impressed with how he respected the students. I saw the swollen abdomens of pregnancies and the misplaced bravado displayed by some of the young men. But even more, I noticed how they responded to Mr. Dixon. They seemed to have welcomed him into their troubled lives. He genuinely cared about them, and I sensed that many of them appreciated the Friendship—or Relationship— he walked, shared, and taught into their lives.

Your role beyond instruction, your Friendship, can be the catalyst that makes a difference for the future community trustees in your school.

CHAPTER 8

Brotherhood

The Fifth Habit of the Heart

An Intentional Principle

*In our schools, Brotherhood is the habit that
reaches beyond comfortable relationships to extend a
welcome to those who may be different from ourselves.*

W ith Nurturing Attitude, Responsibility, Dependability, and Friendship, you are well on your way to building your ideal school community, where great things and major initiatives can take root and grow, but it won't happen without this habit of the heart, Brotherhood. Brotherhood means reaching beyond our comfort zones to embrace others, to dream big for others, and to celebrate our shared humanity. This habit demands that you reach out to those you may not have considered before as possible friends or colleagues.

Without a doubt, there's a place for Brotherhood in your school, but someone has to bring it to school each day, and that's truer than ever as we experience the diversity of the world population within our neighborhoods and within our schools. Brotherhood should start with the adults, educators who respect and share with each other, extending their relationships beyond the 3 P.M. bell, and becoming a community of school employees working toward a single goal. If we want our students to extend their concern beyond a small clique of closest friends, then so must we as adults. Students need to see Brotherhood lived out in front of them, and adults need to experience its presence.

Due to the restrictions posed by the system of legal segregation, my school did not enjoy the benefits that come from reaching beyond comfort to someone unlike yourself. As you can imagine, in the 1950s and 1960s, extending a welcome to people different from oneself was a rare opportunity—and sometimes, a significant risk. At my little school in Glen Allan, Mississippi, Brotherhood was simply a conversation about the future, not a present reality.

However, building relationships that reach beyond comfort zones is a requirement for educational success today. The world has changed, and all of its residents are becoming our neighbors. Nowhere is this more evident than within our schools. If you are to maximize your educational opportunity and maximize your students' learning opportunity, then you must lead the way in creating school environments where all are respected, affirmed, and included. Within the classroom, teachers can make a tremendous difference in how this generation of students embraces their opportunity to reach beyond what appears to be comfortable and safe and discover the rewards of a life shared with people different from themselves.

When I was a boy, it was important for me to experience Brotherhood, and it is important for kids now. There are far more opportunities to reach beyond comfort now, but it is no less challenging. Let me share with you the story that continues to mean Brotherhood to me.

✐ From the Front Porch

It seems as if it was only yesterday when raking leaves to earn extra money was part of my way of life. Miss Knight, an older white lady who lived uptown, wanted her yard to take on the look of a freshly cleaned green carpet. It became my job to make her dream come true.

When noontime came around, Miss Knight would come out of her sewing shop, look over her yard, and then look at me. "Clifton, well, hurry up," she would say. "It's time to eat." During those days, as a rule, little "colored" boys were not invited into white homes to sit at the table and share food together. For whatever reason, my employer opted not to follow the strict social mores of our town and invited me in to join her for lunch, eating from her china and drinking from her crystal.

"Come on, Clifton," she would say. "Follow me."

And I would follow Miss Knight, who walked fast, her white hair piled atop her head and her ever-present shawl dragging on the ground even in the heat and humidity of the Mississippi Delta. She would lead me through her living room to the dining room where we sat down to lunch, the menu rarely changing. There was baked chicken, sweet milk (milk straight from the cow), light bread (packaged bread purchased from the grocery store), and slow-cooked lima beans from local gardens. We ate, and we talked. Miss Knight always encouraged me to complete school and go on to college. I never felt as if I was being groomed to rake her fig leaves for the rest of my life.

Follow me. Brotherhood implies a journey of more than one. When Miss Knight said "follow me," she set in motion the path of right travel. Your actions among students and fellow educators should also say "follow me."

However, this simple phrase may be difficult to say and even more difficult to do if you allow your journey to become burdened with prior learning that devalues others. It's difficult to ask people we do not value to join us. It's no different within our schools. You must strive to become Brotherhood, not only for the adults you encounter but for the students who will get their signals from your actions. Standing at your door, sitting at your desk, walking among your students, or simply getting out of your car and finding your way to your job, your actions are providing a model for your students. You'll often find students doing what they see you do.

> Think of an experience in childhood when you reached "beyond comfort."
>
> Do you reach beyond comfort today? How?

I needed to see Brotherhood lived out by an adult. In our strictly segregated world, small reaches could have enormous impact, and Miss Knight's action made a powerful impression on me. Back then, her invitation to follow her was a rare instance of an adult practicing Brotherhood in the presence of an impressionable young boy. The world I knew as a child no longer exists; however, the need to reach beyond comfort zones still does. And this is especially true within our schools, both urban and suburban. Students need you, the adult with authority and position, to validate for them the reasons why we reach out to others. It's perfectly all right for educators to let students see them being intentionally unselfish among themselves and among all the adults who contribute daily to the educational process. It brings dividends to the student who observes and to the adult who has the experience.

Reaching out is necessary, not only in the classroom but on the playground and the athletic fields, within the teachers' lounge, anywhere in the school. Teachers and other school employees must reach out and embrace each other as the first step in ensuring the presence of this dynamic habit in your school. Your students need to see this type of unselfishness to embrace its value.

Brotherhood is an invitation. The first step in making the reach beyond comfort is to accept and embrace our shared humanity. Miss Knight did this, recognizing that eating was as important to me as it was to her. Hunger was something we had in common, and understanding our commonalities is an important aspect of Brotherhood.

The heart of Brotherhood is reaching beyond comfort and extending a welcome to someone who may be different from you: stretching your table, as Miss Knight did. I know that you can become this habit of the heart and give Brotherhood life within your school because I saw it happen in a place and time when people boasted that Brotherhood did not exist. In those days when my employer and I ate together in her home, it was socially unacceptable to do so. We were together in our workplace where we each had a job to do, and Miss Knight's unselfish act of stretching her dining room table became the reality of a "human touch" I experienced yesterday that still affects me today.

This seemingly simple unselfish act continues to remind me of the value of this habit of the heart. Give some thought to how you can position yourself to include others in your daily life—or talk about it with your fellow educators.

Bringing Brotherhood into your school can change the relationship dynamics and positively impact the learning process. When your students feel welcomed and included, they will be more likely to establish cross-cultural relationships and less likely to build the type of artificial barriers that could lead to behavior challenges, disruptive classrooms, and low achievement.

> The first time you were invited to reach beyond comfort, how did you react?
>
> When and where did you first practice Brotherhood? And who was the beneficiary of your unselfish act?
>
> What can you do immediately to put this habit into practice in your school?
>
> Do you have a plan of action to keep you on track in building relationships across boundaries?

As an educator, you can become the Miss Knight in your students' lives as well as in the lives of those with whom you work. Students and colleagues will emulate the way you act toward them and the way they see you interact with the variety of people who populate their schools. This reach beyond comfort goes far beyond race and age. It is also important that you reach out to embrace people who are in positions below yours—and those in higher positions, as well. You'll recall the story of my elementary school janitor, Mr. Powell. Our principals and teachers included him as part of the educational team, and that affected how we as young students related to him. This kind of unselfish reach is necessary if you are to fully experience your ideal teaching-learning community.

As I write about the importance of extending a welcome to those who are different from ourselves and how important this is for educators to do, I am reminded of the noted African American scientist George Washington Carver who said,

How different life would be if only I knew you and you knew me.

Dr. Carver needed others to reach beyond their comfort, and he sought to extend that reach to others. Born in slavery, he was originally called Carver's George. In several significant situations, the color of his skin and the circumstance of his birth did not keep others from reaching beyond their comfortable circumstances to extend a welcome to him. Nor did he resist extending a welcome to them, a welcome that eventually led him to college and his subsequent profession of teaching and scientific research. His life as a teacher was one of reaching beyond comfort, as illustrated in his friendship with the automobile magnate Henry Ford. Both men reached beyond their comfort zones to establish a lasting relationship.

Several Carver biographies speak volumes about the relationships that resulted from all this reaching—from others toward him and from him toward others. We see many instances of the tremendous benefits resulting from Brotherhood being lived out. His important discoveries about the benefits hidden within the common peanut constitute only a small part of his legacy. Throughout his life, the Brotherhood he engendered can be seen for all to admire and emulate.

Brotherhood depends on three elements: respecting others, affirming others, and including others. Incorporating these three qualities of human interaction will build a community in which people get to know each other and thus experience the "different life" to which Dr. Carver alluded. Despite the times in which he lived, Dr. Carver showed us what can happen when we embrace our common humanity and celebrate our diversity as our sustaining strength.

No conversation about educators reaching out can be complete without sharing one more timeless historical example, this one left by the noted educator Dr. Mary McLeod Bethune. In addition to being known as a great conversationalist, Dr. Bethune was also known for her tenacity and vision, and she will be remembered for her ability to "stretch tables," her own and the tables of others. In Dr. Bethune's life, First Lady Eleanor Roosevelt played the role of Miss Knight, going beyond the social restrictions of the day to have Dr. Bethune as a trusted and respected friend, as an equal, at her table. Experiencing this reach and enjoying this stretched table enabled Dr. Bethune to maximize her potential for the benefit of countless thousands.

I think how much better my own life might have been if my teachers had been able to forge relationships across lines of difference for themselves and for us. Fortunately, times have changed. In this century, you are positioned to forge honest relationships at your school and to show your students the value of doing so. Your daily actions within your school can define you as Brotherhood.

When I was a young boy, everyone seemed to view the teacher as an extension of our homes, the professional who could help our parents and caretakers realize their dreams for me. It hasn't changed. Teachers, and all who work in schools, are still the much-needed professionals. Without your dedication and commitment to reaching beyond comfort, schools just might not achieve their more noble objective of creating a civil society.

Intentional Strategies to Promote Brotherhood

In our schools, Brotherhood is the habit that reaches beyond comfortable relationships to extend a welcome to those who may be different from ourselves.

- Leave your comfort zone and learn what each child needs to excel.
- Visit students in their homes, and join them in activities outside of school to help develop and cultivate their abilities.
- Build cross-cultural relationship skills through extracurricular activities and other social groups within your school, in which students and adults are encouraged to participate.
- Promote relationships through peer tutoring or cooperative learning activities.
- Be consistent in your treatment of all students. Expose them to a variety of literature, speakers, and other programs that will let them compare themselves to other people, and point out that we are all alike at a basic level.
- Spend time helping students find out what they have in common with others in class. Create common goals and require groups to work together as teams to achieve them.
- Mentor a child in your school.
- Involve students in community service projects.
- Sit with somebody different at staff meetings.

These strategies for using the timeless and universal tool of Brotherhood to build community within classrooms and schools were developed by other educators. Stop and think of several additional strategies that you'd like to see added to this list, strategies that speak specifically to your school's objectives for excellence.

Opportunity to Promote Brotherhood in Your School

Create projects in the classroom and cooperative projects including students from different classes that will require the natural talents and gifts of students from different backgrounds.

- Encourage them to learn from each other in order to complete the projects.
- Arrange the projects in ways that ensure that students of all ethnicities and both genders have the opportunity to become the knowledge source.
- When possible, use parents as resources for the project completion.

Educators Just Like You . . . and Brotherhood

I got to know Camille Narin, a fellow southerner working in South Carolina, through our participation in Boston University's Center for the Advancement of Ethics and Character, which runs summer academies for character development for the state of South Carolina. As South Carolina's Character Education Coordinator, Camille goes beyond even southern hospitality to become Brotherhood for the educators of all races and social statuses who attend the conferences.

She goes out of her way to make sure that each teacher, no matter what school or district he or she represents, feels like the honored guest. I witnessed her continuous efforts to ensure that all her teachers felt included and welcomed. And because she did, others were challenged to follow suit. She welcomes guest professors from other regions to the South she loves and makes the home folks feel that extra warmth, too.

Some educators, especially those from rural and poor districts, may not be expecting such treatment, but Camille Narin makes no distinctions in her relationships with the participants. She sets the standards for Brotherhood and defines it every single day. Her staff from the state office follows her lead, and so do we. Because of her attention to relationship, adult learning benefits.

As educators, you, too, can set the standards. By your practical commitments lived out daily, you bring others into this circle of Brotherhood. We all benefit in such a place.

CHAPTER 9

High Expectations

The Sixth Habit of the Heart

An Intentional Principle

*In our schools, High Expectations involve
believing that others can be successful, telling
them so, and praising their accomplishments.*

I could hardly wait to get to this habit of the heart, High Expectations. It has made the difference in my life and continues to do so. More than anything else, this habit of the heart allows me to bring to your attention the importance of the educator's voice of validation in the Mississippi of my youth and in today's schools.

I believe that many of you are drawn to jobs in education because you love children, you are exhilarated by their potential for growth, and you understand how important their growth is to the future of society. Miss Maxey understood this, and so did Miss Johnnie Mae Harris, teachers from my youth. They stood on the threshold of my future and, with their voices, showed me a different view of myself, one that carved out my place within the broader community. This type of "beyond the plan" vision is still needed. We need the family of educators, from the superintendents to the last staff person hired, to embrace the opportunity to touch others for the future. Parents and the communities in which they live expect a great deal from their schools, and we will meet the goals they set for us to the degree that we have High Expectations of their children.

In this book, I have referred several times to the vision educators must have of their students and who they can become. That vision is at the center of High Expectations. The great artist Michelangelo was asked about the challenge of working with what was, to the natural eye, an oversize piece of stone with no real value. It has been said that Michelangelo responded by saying, "I focused on the angel that I saw and chipped away at the stone until the angel was set free."

I encourage each of you at all levels of the educational process to keep your vision positively focused. While information about a student's demographic characteristics and social or cultural background may prove useful in assessing any potential barriers to education and in selecting appropriate instructional materials and tools, such information should never cause us to lower the bar before we ask this student to jump. Let your vision and expectations chip away at all the unnecessary surroundings so that an engaged student emerges. Every student deserves a chance to be the very best there is.

In America, we often assume that reading, writing, and a vision for the future will be part of a child's environment from infancy, but for some young people, schools are the first place where they are exposed to this incredible world of self-discovery, self-reliance, and personal independence. As an educator, you are in a unique position to welcome that student to that world. Your view of students and your thoughts about who they can become will better equip them to compete with their peers, who may have had more fortunate early years. Accomplishing this is vital to our civilized society, which always reflects individual journeys. The students in our schools are the trustees of our future. We can't go forward without the skills of every single one.

In the Mississippi Delta, High Expectations were a feature of education across several generations, always brought forward by an unselfish individual who relished the opportunity to extract the best from others and then to celebrate their success, which in fact also became the individual's very own. The first of these was an educator who came into the Delta at the start of the 20th century. Although he had retired from education well before I reached school, his reputation for High Expectations was still being discussed when I was a boy, and his impact was still being felt.

✍ From the Front Porch

Old Professor White was almost a god to our grandparents in Glen Allan, Mississippi. He was the "colored" teacher who ignored all the negative conversations about our parents' generation and sought to show the world all the treasure that could be found in the hearts and minds of African American students.

You see, Professor White planted the seeds for the idea that Glen Allan's children could—and should—go far beyond the eighth grade. While plantation owners wanted only a harvest of brawny young men to work in the fields,

Professor White was busy holding a conversation with their parents about an entirely different future. At the time, completing the eighth grade could be a major chore—and sometimes a great accomplishment; Professor White was talking about college, even graduate school.

Parents and students listened. In small Glen Allan, Professor White's efforts and inspiration produced the first doctorate, among "coloreds" or whites, Dr. Sidney S. Boose, my great-aunt's son. As a result of these accomplishments, Professor White was so respected in our community that when he returned for a final visit long after he retired, the whole town turned out to celebrate. Mama Ponk, my great-aunt, was among those who welcomed him back, and so I was there to witness the event and to sit up close as he relived his dream for the youth he had taught. You see, while others might celebrate what he had done, I remember his eyes shining and his face beaming as he celebrated the accomplishments of the youngsters he had been privileged to teach.

How much impact do social data about your students have on your educational style?

How do you show respect for communities defined as nonfunctional?

Do you allow negative comments about students or fellow educators to impact your behavior toward them?

What is your reputation among your students and your peers?

Professor White left a legacy that passed through my parents' generation into my own. Because of his High Expectations for them, a foundation was in place so that my teachers could have High Expectations for me. Like all the others, this habit sends out ripples that make its impact and its value virtually timeless.

When I think of High Expectations during my own school years, I tend to think about Miss Freddye Clay Moore, whose voice—and more important, her constant conversations about what she expected for us—lives vividly in my memory.

🐚 From the Front Porch

In our small cotton-growing community, Miss Moore always dressed impeccably, and she encouraged all of us to do the same. Sometimes, the dress code in communities like Glen Allan didn't suggest an exalted vision of the future for its residents, but Miss Moore paid that no mind.

Rather, Miss Moore visited our small homes and shared her dreams of our abilities with our parents. As she lived it, High Expectations was a way of thinking about others. My mother was always called Mary or Mary Ester, but when Miss Moore came to our house, seeing us playing in the yard, she asked to speak to *Mrs. Taulbert.* Not many people referred to my mother with such respect, but Miss Moore did. And in that seemingly small act, just by using the respected title of *Mrs.,* she told us our mother was an important person. Moreover, we became Mrs. Taulbert's children—and we were important, too.

Miss Moore had High Expectations for the children of Glen Allan, and she was determined not to let the cotton fields of the Delta where we and our families worked define our future.

When I was growing up, I needed Miss Moore's voice, which extended her profession beyond the classroom, and students today will need yours. Beyond your field of study or your particular job in the school, your voice is of great value to your students: Let it be encouraging and complimentary. Today, all students may not recognize the value of your High Expectations, but seeds planted and nourished grow even after the planter calls it a day. Your High Expectations also create a garden that others can nourish as students move along.

We did better work because our teachers expected us to do so, and so will your students. My computer requires no accolades, no luncheon conversation, no notes of thanks, and no voices of affirmation or

> *What difference can your respectful word make in the life of students?*
>
> *What difference can your respectful word make in the life of their parents?*
>
> *How can your position become a role model for success rather than a barrier to communication?*

encouragement. But I do. You do. And so do the students in your school. Students will work better when they are expected to do well. Even in times of advanced technology, youngsters still need to hear the voices of the adults with whom they share their lives: voices that say we believe in you, we expect you to do well, and we admire your accomplishments.

In Glen Allan, Mississippi, many voices encouraged us to expand our vision of the life we might lead, and not all of them were in our homes or the school. Another voice of High Expectations was that of an old man called Preacher Hurn, who didn't live in Glen Allan but often walked to town—and into our lives.

🐝 From the Front Porch

Preacher Hurn lived alone in a small two-room "shotgun" house (these were small homes with a front and back door aligned so you could look—or shoot—straight through) that was filled with books, not allowing for much else, only an iron bed, a wood-burning stove, and a small washstand. The house was in Issaquena County, in a place historically called the "Colored Colony," which was established by landowning blacks after the Civil War and during the era of Reconstruction. Preacher Hurn was known as a reader and talker, always wanting to engage adults in conversations that had little or nothing to do with manual labor and fieldwork.

Many of the adults thought he was "teched" in the head, a common term suggesting a mental disorder. It was probably his stutters and his obsessive desire for meaningful conversation that earned him that title. Although we children didn't know it at the time, his voice was visionary and filled with High

Expectations for us. He had an entirely different view of who we were and who we could become, and he set out to inform our elders and us.

Preacher Hurn usually showed up on Saturdays, dressed in his vested pinstriped gray wool suit and a tie big enough to serve as a chest protector. He wore a hat and carried a satchel filled with books, which he would use to try to gather an audience of children. Because he had no car, he walked to Glen Allan, and by the time he got to our neighborhood, he would be sweating and very thirsty.

Fortunately for me, he always stopped at my great-grandfather's house, where we children would often be in the front yard shooting marbles, the computer game of my times. We all knew Preacher Hurn, and we responded to him with respect and listened as he stuttered his need for a drink of water. My grandpa brought him a dipper filled with chipped ice and cold water, which Preacher Hurn gulped down almost in one continuous swallow. Then, he stopped where we were playing and began to share with us the books he had read.

We listened, but I can't remember much of what he said. I do remember him telling my grandfather that he had read books showing the growth and strength of the "colored" communities and that in spite of what anyone thought, he knew that we children had a promising future. He stuttered out his vision for us while we played with marbles under the hot Delta sun and told us in no uncertain terms that "we were marked for good." And through his talk, he helped the community's adults to see us children from a different perspective—one that included success.

You can become Preacher Hurn for your students—and his conversation is certainly still needed in your school and within your class. The cotton fields of my parents' generation filled my range of vision, but many of my teachers and neighbors lifted my sights beyond the Delta as they prepared me—and the children I grew up with—to

Have another look at the children in your school. Who do you see?

How can you help them to grow beyond their social and geographical limitations?

What is your plan to lift students higher than they can imagine themselves to be?

become the voice of High Expectations for the students of our generation. It's no different today for many of our urban youth and for poorer students from rural areas. Their vision of the future may be negative, one that does not maximize their potential. Educators are still needed today to help change negative pictures and lift expectations.

The voices and actions of High Expectations are always needed: in my parents' time, in my own youth, in this new century, and beyond. Whatever the advancements of technology, your voice as an educator can keep this historical role of building excellence on the move. In spite of the obstacles you may face as educators burdened with extra responsibilities,

- Believe in your students.
- Tell them your positive thoughts.
- Plan to praise their accomplishments.
- Remind them that they are the future trustees of our society.

Intentional Strategies to Promote High Expectations

- Create a positive-behavior bulletin board in the classroom, display a list of children and their positive behaviors on it, and celebrate those youngsters whose names are displayed.
- Create a behavior grade by building it from good behaviors, not by taking away from it due to negative behaviors.
- Adopt a student with low self-esteem and plan to maintain contact.
- Plan activities that will allow a student to experience a measure of success.

(Continued)

- Make praise for students and other teachers more than a onetime event. Build it into your daily plan. It may become contagious.
- Thoroughly explain learning concepts, model them where appropriate, and let students practice them.
- Develop a plan to display the positive works of students and encourage others to follow suit.

These strategies for using the timeless and universal tool of High Expectations to build community within classrooms and schools were developed by other educators. Stop and think of several additional strategies that you'd like to see added to this list, strategies that speak specifically to your school's objectives for excellence.

Opportunity to Promote
High Expectations in Your School

Establish a regular 15-minute confidence-building session during which students are asked to speak out on topics that have meaning for them. Encourage other teachers to do likewise, and at some point share student talks beyond the classroom. Such an activity can make High Expectations a shared experience, one that is on the road, bringing others along.

Educators Just Like You . . . and High Expectations

Steve Thornhill thought his students deserved to be prized, and he wanted to provide them with a priceless education, even though they had been taken out of mainstream schools and assigned to the Orange

County Department of Education County Community School, a division of alternative education. That didn't seem to matter to Mr. Thornhill. The picture that was etched in his mind saw a bright future for them, and he built an environment that could give them a different perspective of themselves. He sent e-mails to parents. He called parents. He visited homes, inviting parents to rise to the occasion of great possibilities.

Mr. Thornhill taught these young men and women more than the academic requirements. He put in the extra effort to keep them on track and to get them believing in themselves. He demanded common courtesy from them in return for the respect he showed them. He wrote notes to parents when something good had been accomplished. If students didn't show up for class, he didn't throw up his hands and give up. He listened to his heart and tried to find out why.

He turned their attention to great literature and gave them opportunities to discover a new and provocative side of themselves. Looking beyond their official designations, Mr. Thornhill could see his students handling great literature, and he gave them the opportunity to do so. Why not have them experience the mind of Shakespeare? Should their circumstances prevent their potential movement forward? He thought not, and neither do I.

This approach becomes successful when people in authority—in Mr. Thornhill's case, his immediate supervisor, Mary Lou Vachet—support the effort. High Expectations flourish when the educational team recognizes this value and embraces their collective opportunity to use High Expectations to support their students.

Some would ask why a teacher would waste such efforts when students' backgrounds are sending a different signal of requirements. Steve Thornhill, however, received his signals from the future, one that students were crafting in his presence, and with the support of his administration, he has shown his commitment to protect all his students from negativity and mistreatment.

CHAPTER 10

Courage

The Seventh Habit of the Heart

An Intentional Principle

*In our schools, Courage is standing up and
doing the right thing, speaking out on behalf
of others, and making a commitment to excellence
in the face of adversity or the absence of support.*

At first glance, it may not seem to you that individual acts of Courage are required as part of everyday work at schools in 21st-century America. Many schools have so many amenities, and even in our challenging educational environment, we have moved beyond many of the inequities of the 20th century. So why do I offer you Courage as part of your 21st-century education package?

First, it's important to recognize that Courage is not a mere concept; for our purposes, Courage is an unselfish person who has vision beyond his or her personal world and is determined to remove the obstacles that would keep that vision from becoming a reality. Doesn't this describe the committed educator? Courage shows up in many forms, and we see all kinds of Courage, but it is always introduced and embodied by a person. The journey of education in America has been marked by men and women who because of their unselfish vision were determined to create new and inclusive models, often pushing the cart uphill. America and, need I say, the world have been beneficiaries of such Courage.

As we recognize the value of education, we must remember to position it as foundational to democracy. Courage is required for this process. Likewise, Courage is required within schools to keep both educators and students focused on education when faced with low pay, social disruptions, and overwhelming legislative mandates. When you become Courage, you travel beyond limitations, whether they're imposed by others or by yourself.

In today's schools, educators have opportunities to show all kinds of Courage. Sadly, in some school settings, violence poses a real threat to personal safety, or apathy among political and educational leaders may leave schools without the resources they need. In those cases, educators must have the Courage to take action against those who pose a danger and to stand up and demand what is needed so that students can learn.

Even when the actual violence remains outside of the school building, it may sneak inside disguised in the fears and personal traumas experienced by some students, experiences that reduce their expectations and get in the way of learning. These students need a courageous person to hold their hands and hearts and give them strength.

Your school day may also feature a daunting array of requirements for assessment and testing, combined with budgetary restrictions that make it feel nearly impossible to make do with what you have. It takes Courage to persist through these trials.

Courage is not an abstraction. It has always been a person willing to rise to the occasion, and it always involves risks. Courage rewards not only those who practice it but those who witness it as well. Your show of Courage reminds your students that it is still a worthy quality to possess. When they see it lived out through you, it becomes more than a reference to a historical figure or a movie hero. Students can stand back and see its impact. Courage comes alive as a present-day principle, one that they might emulate. Your students as well as your fellow educators need to experience someone motivated by unselfishness to stand up and speak out, even when it appears as if no one has your back.

When I was growing up in Glen Allan, Mississippi, the racism and segregation of the times provided too many opportunities for Courage, and the adults around me always seemed ready to step forward and do what was required. The Courage I witnessed involved real people motivated by an unselfish vision for their children, including me. They faced danger and violence, they stood by us in difficult times, and they kept moving forward—and moving their children ahead—despite their limited resources. Let me tell you about Spike Ayers.

🐦 From the Front Porch

Spike Ayers lived outside the box. He was Courage with salt-and-pepper hair that framed his weatherworn face. I knew him all my life. Spike Ayers was one of those men who saw the big picture and recognized that education was the key to the future of the young people he encountered on a daily basis. He was a friend to our teachers and regarded them highly. He got to know them and, in so doing, became well aware of their plight.

As the 1960s and the civil rights movement moved into small-town Mississippi, Spike Ayers and other men and women like him were in the forefront, galvanizing people to seek alternative ways to level the playing field for their children. He became the look of Courage as he set forth to shift the educational paradigm in our county and our small community. Before it was acceptable, he was standing up for the children who were being left behind on a regular basis. He wanted and fought for early educational intervention before first grade. Many people thought this was a waste of money—and a particular waste when the money was allocated to African Americans for their teachers and their children.

A price is often paid for standing up and speaking out . . . and Spike Ayers paid severely for his stance. He became a target for the Ku Klux Klan, and he was stopped and beaten on our Highway 1 for his unselfish vision. He survived the beating and the burning crosses, with his Courage intact. He was still fighting on our behalf when he died in 1985.

> *What causes such Courage to surface at just the right times?*
>
> *Do you recognize the value of doing the right thing for your students, even if others—including those with the power to cause you trouble—are doing differently?*
>
> *How do you reward students who stand up for what is right?*

Spike Ayers showed the kind of Courage most people think of first when this habit of the heart is mentioned. Certainly, it took great Courage to do what he did, knowing that he risked physical injury and even death. But it always takes Courage to stand up for what is right when others disagree—especially when those others are in positions of authority. How do you employ Nurturing Attitude, Responsibility, Dependability, Friendship, and High Expectations to influence the people whose support your courageous acts will need?

This is why we ask you to focus on building community among all educators as a way of life and work. At times, your peers may need to reflect on your previous actions and on your mutual bonds as they contemplate your present-day stand. The consistency of your voice will go a long way in persuading others to support you or at least to minimize the potential opposition. Community is the environment we build in anticipation of such times.

The people of my small "colored" community were often overlooked by the broader society; for the most part, nothing was expected of them except manual labor. Yet they had the Courage to struggle against the reach of segregation, the ever-present spoiler. They stood on their front porches and kept watch, so that we their children could have a future of expanded opportunities. As educators, you do this each day. You are the visionaries on the front porches of their lives, looking out for students of whom others may expect little. The history of your journey as educators has shown you the unlimited possibilities your students represent. The fabric that defines this country is woven with stories of educators who inspired their students. Just like Miss Maxey on my first day, you still work the magic that, over time, can turn a small scared boy into the fuel that powers this incredible economy. As educators, you continue to be your students' advocate, to stand up for their right to pursue their potential. Your lesson plans become the reflection of your commitment to seeing them prepared for an ever-changing society.

Through their daily acts of Courage, my first teachers hacked away at the tentacles of legal segregation and limited its reach. As you think about your classroom and your school environment, what acts of Courage by you and your colleagues could paint a brighter picture for your students? Without question, I needed the Courage of my teachers and other community elders to move my life along a path that society may not have had in mind for me. You have students on your watch who need that same type of Courage to help them navigate their way to a bright future. Sometimes, all they need is a hand to hold on to and eyes that say welcome.

🕮 From the Front Porch

It took Courage for my Poppa Joe to take me to Greenville, knowing full well that we were not welcome there. He never told me about the situation. All I recall is getting dressed and waiting for my great-grandfather to come out on the front porch to start the process. On those Saturday mornings when we were going to Greenville, it seemed as if time stood still, and there was nothing I could do to move it along. Instead of being fast, Poppa seemed to shave slower than ever, and I thought his soap-covered face might never again be the wonderful shiny black face I had come to love. He eventually finished, and we were off to the city, me and my best friend.

The ride up old Highway 1 was long and, from my perspective, filled with adventure as I named everything along the way. When we finally passed the monkey store (a general merchandise store where pet monkeys were kept), I knew I was close to Greenville. I could almost smell the delicacies that awaited me on Washington Avenue.

But Washington Avenue held more than the smells I craved. It was also a place where legal segregation was practiced and legally enforced. Poppa knew this all too well, but he never spoiled the joy of my anticipation. We might have to step off the sidewalk while members of a different race briskly walked by, ignoring our presence. Although he was unable to legally challenge the system that interfered with our lives, he stood up for me, holding tight to my hand as we walked down Washington Avenue, and in so doing, he held my heart. I saw the world through the strength of his touch and the Courage of his heart.

Having to move off the sidewalk to let others pass was a fact of life for "colored" people in those days. However, what I remember more is my great-grandfather's grip on my hand. It was not a small act, but one of great proportion to a young boy. His act of unselfish Courage told me that I had worth and value, so much so that he put his feelings on hold to take care of my heart. I dread to think the course of my life had Poppa not been so courageous.

Against the obstacles that some of your students face—both personal disadvantage and institutional factors—you may feel that "holding a hand" is of little value. I will tell you, though, that your small and consistent acts of Courage can have as much impact as legislative acts and funding vehicles might have. Because Poppa Joe held my hand, I continued to walk toward the object of my anticipation and Poppa's dream for my future. Your students will benefit not only on the day you take their hands but far beyond. I know this to be true. I still feel Poppa's big calloused hands lovingly holding mine. Stopping to hold a heart takes Courage, even when there is no crisis. Keep doing it. Courage needs you.

✌ From the Front Porch

When I think of Courage, I also think of Mr. A. J. Moore, our principal. The impact of legal segregation went beyond the separation of the races. Within the separate systems, legal segregation sought to further erode our quest for excellence by providing us, the "colored" students, with out-of-date and used textbooks. As if it were only yesterday, I can see the old truck from the white school pulling up to our school and unloading old books. We were expected to be excited.

As I watched and listened, our teachers handled each book as if it was the most up-to-date text ever seen, never communicating to us their level of disappointment. We were taught to ignore the scribbling on the worn pages and to embrace the truth of the knowledge that was before us. From those often-torn and worn pages, our teachers brought to life great lessons and sought ways to supplement what Mr. Moore and his teachers knew we were missing. Mr. Moore stood up for us and taught beyond the obvious slight. He became Courage in our midst.

Poppa Joe, Miss Maxey, Mr. Moore, Miss Ross, Mr. Powell (our janitor), and others held our hands and protected our image of ourselves. They were driven by a much bigger picture than a little boy could see, one that wasn't in tune with the times. My teachers had the Courage to hold on to this picture of success and to make sure I saw myself through their eyes. This century also needs educators who have the Courage see their students' possibilities, even when everyone around them is talking about their limitations. As an educator, your vision must also extend beyond the image students may have of themselves.

> When did you last experience an act of Courage within your school?
>
> What was your reaction to an act of Courage demonstrated by one of your peers?
>
> How can you be a courageous educator for your students?

Some may tell you that it's a waste of time and energy to try to promote students who come from poor families and disadvantaged neighborhoods. The zip code, however, is intended to facilitate delivery of the mail, not to brand our children. Don't let their demographics determine your educational style. Educators are needed who have the Courage to see that the best of American education must be available to all students. Building a community of like-minded people who embrace each other's dreams makes fertile ground for Courage to take root and be lived out in our presence.

Having Courage requires building relationships—slowing down to know those on your watch. Because our elders in Glen Allan—and, yes, our teachers—knew us, it was more natural for them to step up and speak out on our behalf. We were not strangers anyplace we went in our community. Among the adults in my small world, our common humanity had been established as the link that would bind us together. As they got to know us and welcomed us into their world, their future became entangled with ours; thus, bonds were established that would make our march toward success their march as well.

Getting to know your students and being connected to their lives will impact your ability to step up and out on their behalf. Just make sure that when you connect, you connect with all, not just the bright and the gifted. It may take Courage on your part to stretch to this level, but your history as American educators proves that you can do this. When you know people and feel a sense of kinship, standing up for them becomes easier. When your dreams are intimately tied to your students' dreams, you will stand up and speak out on their behalf if anything puts those dreams in jeopardy.

In our schools and classrooms, young people still need adults to value them enough that they are willing to hold their hands and hearts when seemingly nothing else can be done. Stuff happens in life and in schools. It takes Courage to hold hands and look beyond old and worn textbooks. It takes Courage to keep your students focused when it seems as if the system has written them off. You must never forget who your students are. Even if they have never known their role in our society, you know it and must never forget. Our students are America's trustees, and your courageous stance on their behalf is needed.

Keep in mind that when this habit is embraced, more than good grades will result. Grades are important. They are an acceptable indicator of effort and progress. Seeing, experiencing, and becoming Courage is also important. Educators, I encourage you to embrace your front-row position to ensure that your students see Courage each and every day. In a free society, Courage is an essential part of the educational process. Courage will in no way guarantee you a certificate of achievement, but because of your unselfish and bold stand, students will recall with clarity how an educator they once knew held their hands when there was little else that could be done.

Intentional Strategies to Promote Courage

In our schools, Courage is standing up and doing the right thing, speaking out on behalf of others, and making a commitment to excellence in the face of adversity or the absence of support.

(Continued)

(Continued)

- Encourage children to listen to and follow their inner voices when opportunities arise in the classroom or at school, and use those opportunities to discuss and develop their consciousness.
- Advocate quality education for all students within your state in the face of legislation and political fads that make this difficult to achieve.
- Plan activities that allow students to share life experiences that show the importance of Courage, and share courageous experiences of your own.
- Portray Courage in the classroom by not backing down when parents try to force you to give students grades they don't deserve.
- Find a way to bring a wrong action to the attention of the right people, even it means offending another person or facing the possible loss of relationships.
- Consider doing what is best for the child no matter what.

These strategies for using the timeless and universal tool of Courage to build community within classrooms and schools were developed by other educators. Stop and think of several additional strategies that you'd like to see added to this list, strategies that speak specifically to your school's objectives for excellence.

Opportunity to Promote Courage in Your School

Consider assigning several students on a rotating basis to become the social advocates for students whose cultures might be hindering them from full participation in the school. As these new students become more comfortable, add them to the social advocacy team for others. Discuss the learning and relationship that result from students who become Courage for others who otherwise might be left on the outside looking in.

⚜ Educators Just Like You . . . ⚜ and Courage

Courage often allows educators not only to think outside of the box but also to take positive steps that may fly in the face of tradition. Many southern states had some difficult moments during the transition from separate-but-equal education to a system that embraced all. Alabama and its school systems were also challenged to embrace a changing social pattern. Indeed, Alabama made national news in its attempt to hold education hostage to the past. However, the tides of change would come, and courageous Alabama educators of both races would rise to the occasion and embark on building good community.

Ensuring good community makes deep and personal demands, which often require Courage to follow through, and this can be especially true when the past is not so easily left behind. However, there are always those who, by their Courage and unselfishness, lead the way for others. I think in particular of Nancy Grisham Anderson, Professor of English at Auburn University at Montgomery, Alabama. Professor Anderson embodied Courage as the power of literature moved her beyond the college walls to make sure that secondary educators, many often overlooked, were aware that they too could avail themselves of this habit of Courage for themselves and for their students. As she and a friend reflected on speeches by me and by author Pat Conroy, discussing *The Water Is Wide,* they were moved to action:

[We felt] that powerful speeches by two such dynamic individuals should not be just events but should make a real difference in our lives, if not in the life of the university. More personally, in the tradition of my father, a Methodist minister who spoke out during the civil rights movement, I realized that I had to do more than just listen and talk; I had to take some action. That conversation led to other conversations and a specific proposal: a course in literature and community to be offered on the campus of AUM and at two public high schools in Montgomery in the fall of 1997. . . .

The course was designed with two specific goals: first, students would read, write about, and discuss works that took them into communities they did not know; and, second, students had to perform five hours of community service each week, working on projects about which they would write and which they would discuss with the class. The reading lists varied from school to school . . . covering subjects as varied as civil rights, education, spousal abuse, child neglect and abuse, AIDS, poverty, justice—and the list can go on.

Many of the class's participants have been inspired to help those less privileged than themselves, reaching beyond traditions of the past, Professor Anderson says. For many of these students, Courage was absolutely necessary to answer this call, Professor Anderson continued,

A young woman selecting a career of serving special children, students working in soup kitchens and nursing homes, college students and athletes becoming passionate about a program where they can make a difference. Who knows what differences they have made in the lives of the children they have already met?

Like all the habits of the heart, Courage has enormous power. Its impact may live for many years and extend well beyond the goals of the person who stepped forward and spoke out.

CHAPTER 11

Hope

The Eighth Habit of the Heart

An Intentional Principle

*In our schools, Hope is believing in
tomorrow—going beyond what we see
because we have learned to see with our hearts.*

You are Hope. Your voice, your expectations, your vision, your commitment—all of your efforts to be the best educator you can be—all of these ensure the presence of Hope in your school. Students from past generations benefited from the presence of this habit of the heart, and so will the students you currently serve. Unless Hope is personalized for your students, many of them will not be able to take their educational journey to its most promising destination.

All educators are futurists. You are driven by your belief that you are investing knowledge for a future return. Just as Miss Maxey stood at the front door welcoming me, not just to school but to a future of possibilities, teachers still stand at the threshold of young lives welcoming their students to a journey into their own potential. Educators have not changed. Thank you for being at the front door.

Without question, your belief in tomorrow is evident in your commitment to the rigorous and often challenging requirements of your profession. From court cases to governmental requirements, you are being bombarded with extra duty and more paperwork than you signed on to handle. However, most of you have not forgotten why you chose to pursue a career in education. The needs of your students—and your Hope for them, your Hope for the future of society—continue to drive your efforts.

Students may be unaware of your extra workload; they may not understand how badly you want them to succeed—or why. Although they may want to slack off and do less, you continue to push them toward excellence because the Hope you embody for them shows you a different picture. As my teachers were for me, you are Hope, standing in front of the class, walking the aisle and leaning over shoulders, inspecting homework, and often providing that extra pat on the shoulder that motivates.

When I was growing up during the 1950s and 1960s, I encountered adults and teachers who challenged us to do our best; they acted as if the whole world could hardly wait to embrace our achievements when, in fact, there were those who cared little for us. Our teachers ignored the fact that the mental capacity of "colored" people was still a matter of intellectual debate, and America is better because they did. As my teachers did in the era of Jim Crow, you need to look beyond the socially debilitating rhetoric of our times—as I did then, your students need you to do so now.

When Hope is in the air, life-changing events are likely to take place. I saw that happen not once but many times in the biography of my mother, Mary Morgan Taulbert.

From the Front Porch

In our small cotton-growing community, my mother was remembered by several educators as having a special gift to work with people and with children. She had established herself as a well-respected plantation school teacher, involving both parents and the community in the educational process. I recall those years when Mother taught at the Peru Plantation School and all the children and parents who were involved.

I also recall when my mother no longer taught school, due to personal circumstances. It had been years since she was in a classroom, and she hadn't bothered to maintain her teacher certification. Turned aside from that rewarding work, my mother had become a fieldworker and a maid. All too often, people with great human assets find themselves overburdened and overwhelmed by life circumstances. Like my mother, many turn their backs on promising careers and return to a world they had once wanted so passionately to leave behind.

Fortunately for my mother, Hope showed up in the person of Spike Ayers, whose story depicted Courage in Chapter 10, and Ann Britton, who was one of Washington County's supervisors for the "Negro" teachers. They remembered her talents and looked beyond her present circumstances and invited her to return to the world of her dreams. They became Hope for her.

They rekindled her personal vision. Excited but somewhat reluctant, my mother was persuaded by the power of their belief to make a new start. Mr. Ayers and Miss Britton set out to get her the tools that would help her become the person they envisioned. My mother studied at the University of Alabama, where she excelled, and she met all the state and federal requirements to become an administrator within the Mississippi Head Start System. Shortly thereafter, she became the director of the Yates Head Start Center in Washington County.

My mother was a beneficiary of Hope. When students and adults drop out of the system, they don't always have the good fortune to find someone who will get them back on the road again. Preoccupied by new students and competing interests, educators may forget someone who once showed a spark. Reaching back to give that someone a hand becomes a living teaching moment, not only for those like my mother who are pulled forward but also for everyone who watches the process. They all experience Hope.

> *Can you recall a Mr. Ayers or Miss Britton who gave you a new vision of yourself?*
>
> *Do you remember a time when an educator went above and beyond the call of duty to benefit you?*
>
> *What can you do to encourage students who are languishing in school?*
>
> *How can you show students that they are valuable people, even though the system may have defined them differently?*

Mr. Ayers and Miss Britton embodied Hope for my mother, and soon enough, it was her turn to pass the favor along to others. During the 1960s, she walked into the lives of a group of sharecroppers in the Mississippi Delta and left many of them with a different picture of themselves and their children. She didn't give them a concept paper to ponder or a warm pat on the back. She walked into their restricted world, and through her positive actions, she gave them Hope: the power to go beyond what you see because of what you believe within your heart.

✌ From the Front Porch

The Yates Head Start Center where my mother worked sat in a clearing off the Wayside Road, just a few miles south of Greenville, Mississippi. Surrounded on three sides by cotton fields, the building itself consisted of several farmhouses linked together. It wasn't much to look at, but my mother knew how her life had been changed by people who looked beyond her circumstances and saw a different future for her. She was determined to do the same for this center and the people it served.

After a period of time, the grass was neatly trimmed, and the frame building was painted white. It was harder to transform the sharecroppers and tenant farmers who were my mother's potential clients. For years, the plantation system had given them a distorted view of themselves and their children, and they were reluctant to embrace my mother's vision. My mother, however, was determined. With a new and challenging job, my once shy and retiring mother rose to her full height on behalf of her young students and her staff.

Some parents sent their children to Head Start, but the parents themselves never came to the center. My mother knew she had to find a way to get the adults involved in the educational process so they would reinforce her efforts at home. Parents were invited to events, but they didn't show up. Notes were sent, and they still didn't come. Finally, she decided to begin visiting parents at their homes.

At first, her visits were viewed with suspicion; some people were fearful because, after all, this program to educate the overlooked African American children of fieldworkers was viewed with disdain by many of the plantation owners who employed them. My mother was well aware of these feelings, but her Hope for these families gave her strength.

Sometimes, she remembers, she would stand and knock and stand and knock some more before someone would come and barely open the door. "I am the teacher at Yates," she would say. The adult, often with head cast down, would quickly reply, "I sent my chile." But Mother would say, "I want you to come to the center and see what good work your child is doing." They would banter back and forth, my mother still on the porch; she would stick her hopeful foot in the partially opened door until she was finally invited inside.

Sometimes, Hope is easier to find in schools that come with neatly landscaped neighborhoods and plenty of parent participation. Yet Hope is needed just as much or even more in those neighborhoods where the sidewalks are cracked and grass refuses to grow, where parents work hard but find less time to be actively involved in the school life of their children, or where parents have not embraced the importance of their personal commitment. They just send their children off to school.

When did you put aside the hard facts of what you saw to act on what you believed?

What people need to see you on their doorsteps, encouraging their dreams and ignoring their excuses?

How can you stick a hopeful foot in the door?

Parents are part of the benevolent conspiracy we need to move our children forward to success. Yet many urban families today face the same disheartening circumstances as the fieldworker families of my mother's community. They may feel that education doesn't matter for them or for their children, that nothing will change, that there is no tomorrow. Without the intervention of Hope, they may find no reason to believe.

That, of course, is where educators can and must step in, following in my mother's footsteps. Your Hope—your positive view of what is possible—can persuade children to accept another vision of themselves, and it can enlist their parents' support in this vitally important effort. Of course, parents may not come to school or seek out educators to talk about their children. That doesn't mean that educators are off the hook. You already have a positive vision of your students. Use that vision to extend yourself to their parents. I know it's not always easy to visit the homes of your students, and it may seem, at first, that you are not particularly welcome. It wasn't easy for my mother either.

However, my mother understood that these families were her kin. She may not have known their names, but she knew that they shared common human bonds. This is the view educators need today to build schools where all are respected and included. Hope is persistent because it is motivated by deeply held beliefs in the fact of our common humanity. With such an outlook, anyone's success is intimately tied to *everyone's* success.

You can do this. Here's how my mother managed it.

🐚 From the Front Porch

Once inside a family's small home, where one room often served multiple purposes, she immediately set out to put her host at ease. As my mother saw it, position and place should not be used to separate people. Sensing that the parents saw teachers as part of a different social world, she sought to bridge this artificial barrier by embracing their common humanity—honestly partaking of the parents' lives.

She would ask for a drink of water. While the parent was getting it, she looked for something in the home that would speak to the creative uniqueness of her host, often something that the host's hands had made. And when she did, she quickly asked if it could be used at the center. The parent, usually the mother, was moved by this request, and my mother began the process of lifting the parent's sights by showing that something in the home had value.

My mother was becoming Hope for these families, moved not by what she saw in their present circumstances but by what she knew could be their tomorrow. As a result of her commitment to follow her heart's vision, Yates Center just off Wayside Road became a model of achievement and parental involvement. Although there were no trees to provide shade from the sun, the Yates Center was an inviting place, a haven, for both students and parents.

> How well do you know the parents of your students?
>
> Do they share Hope for their children?
>
> How could you reach out and persuade them to do so?

Hope is not an abstraction. In Glen Allan, Hope was the vision of two people who remembered my mother's gifts, though hidden behind a maid's apron, and persuaded her to change her life. Hope was the invitation my mother, Mary Morgan Taulbert, extended to sharecroppers, her sensitivity to their situation, her gentle efforts to make them feel their worth and, through that, to see a promise for their children. Hope lived in the teachers and their aides who every day welcomed the children of the sharecroppers to the renovated farmhouse turned school just off Wayside Road. And nothing has changed. Hope is still educators making parents and students feel welcome and wanted in today's schools as they make their way into tomorrow.

Although Hope is the eighth of the Eight Habits of the Heart, it is not the end. Hope connects you back to Nurturing Attitude, for through Hope, you may be moved to share your time with your students and with your peers. Hope is the habit that drives you to think unselfishly and to act accordingly. When Hope is brought into your school on a daily basis, you ensure a climate that will connect you and your students to the first habit of the heart, Nurturing Attitude, as well as all the habits between the first and the last.

When Hope is present in your school, electricity is in the air. Expectancy runs rampant. The educational process takes on a positive dimension. Something happens, and everything is different. Students who might otherwise have been slow to step up and perform may see themselves in a more positive light. Your dreams for their future can become their own, and those dreams can create a new reality, not just for your students but for the society they will grow up to lead.

Intentional Strategies to Promote Hope

In our schools, Hope is believing in tomorrow—going beyond what we see because we have learned to see with our hearts.

- Encourage students to set high goals for themselves and become involved in the monitoring and reward process.
- Have students keep journals of what they do each day to achieve their goals; remind them that if they don't reach their goals today, tomorrow will provide another opportunity.
- Tell the students several stories that explain Hope.
- Read biographies that show how someone who starts in modest circumstances can become a great person.
- Develop a classroom or school vision statement and remind the students that they are the reality of that statement.
- Encourage students to run for office, join clubs, and develop their talents.
- Look for the good in others: Find a skill or personality characteristic and encourage them to develop it.
- Speak your encouragement to all students, even to the most resistant students; over time, you may make a dent in their resistance.
- Don't plan on a bad day; start each day with an expectation of accomplishment and collegiality.

These strategies for using the timeless and universal tool of Hope to build community within classrooms and schools were developed by other educators. Stop and think of several additional strategies that you'd like to see added to this list, strategies that speak specifically to your school's objectives for excellence.

Opportunity to Promote Hope in Your School

- Use the teachers' lounge as a resource center where you can draw positive feelings from each other and learn ways to become a safety net of Hope for those students who may not be experiencing this habit of the heart in their homes or among their peers.
- Think of what you can do immediately to be the voice of Hope for someone else, a peer or student.
- Consider what good deed you would do, if you had only one day to make a difference. Then do it.

Educators Just Like You . . . and Hope

Jimmy Hart visits homes. He writes notes. He sends parents e-mails. He holds hands and hearts. He keeps pointing to the vision of success that his heart has embraced for his students. He embodies Hope. Totally unmoved by the fact that at one time many of his students were on the outside of mainstream education, this educator taught and planned beyond what he saw because of what he believed could be.

When I first met Jimmy Hart—a young and distinguished-looking African American in khaki pants and shirt, both starched and pressed— he was working at Oklahoma's Francis Tuttle Vocational Educational Center, which provided an alternative plan for youth who were no longer part of the traditional public school system. Now he is a principal in the Tucson Unified School District in Arizona. His Hope for his youngsters is intertwined with his concept of community and the Eight Habits of the Heart. At one point, while in Oklahoma, he worked for Project HOPE, a dropout recovery program aimed at those students who had dropped out of mainstream education. What I noticed, though, was his commitment to personalize the program. *Hope* was not a reference word for Mr. Hart but his call to action, one he took very seriously. Jimmy Hart became an advocate for his students, and in so doing, he gave them reason to reexamine how they valued themselves. He wanted their tomorrow to be decidedly different but realized that the change he sought for them had to be birthed within their thinking. And his consistent unselfishness would be required to make this transition. Here's how he tells it:

> My objective was to instill within each of my students a sense of purpose and a new vision for themselves—one beyond how they were being defined. Upon being introduced to Mr. Taulbert's concept of community and the Habits required to build and sustain such a community, I immediately brought them into my planning. With support from my superiors at Francis Tuttle, I incorporated the Eight Habits of the Heart as part of a schoolwide curriculum module. . . . With guidance from myself and others, students were assigned readings from the book, *Eight Habits of the Heart,* and were asked to provide think-aloud strategies about what they had read and its applicability to their lives. . . . Were these stories giving them a picture of new possibilities for them? After all this is the objective of Project HOPE.
>
> I found it rewarding to see how these students, many on the verge of walking away from being responsible citizens, were challenged to think more positively of themselves as we went through this curriculum process. Being a young educator at the time, the book was also challenging me to hold fast to my view of how their future could look and who they could become. I realized that I had to become the HOPE I talked about. The Eight Habits leaped from the pages into their thinking; thus impacting their action.

Mr. Hart used the same strategy later in his career, as principal of Whitney Middle School in Tulsa, Oklahoma. Part of his job was to handle disciplinary referrals.

I dealt with this small group of students who were repeat offenders. ... I was again placed in a situation where I had to become HOPE for these students, motivated beyond their repeated negative actions, because of the positive view I held of them. I refused to let their actions dictate my thoughts of who they could become. I had learned this while growing up and it was validated again as I read Mr. Taulbert's book. For these repeat offenders, the Eight Habits became the topic of conversation and discussion two days per week. ... After each vigorous discussion, sometimes with examples from history and current events, they were asked to share with each other how what they had just learned and discussed could be applied to their situation both at school and at their homes. Overtime, as the program continued, we noticed a reduction in the discipline required for these students as they began to slowly embrace the actions that were reflective of the positive view I held for them. Their behavior challenged me, but my belief in them welled up as the HOPE I had to become on their behalf.

As embodied in educators like Mr. Hart, Hope is the magic that can transform troubled youth into promising young men and women. You can give this gift of Hope to the students in your school, too, and then watch how they thrive.

CHAPTER 12

Building Community . . .
Sustaining the Excellence

*We do not extend help to children
solely because of moral obligations. It is
also because we have faith in the future
of our society, in its progress, its values,
and its traditions, and we want our
children to have every possible opportunity to
participate in the society and contribute to it.*

—MARIAN WRIGHT EDELMAN

A t the beginning of this book, we spent some time talking about the importance of building a school community. We also described building community as the blueprint for our educational project. The Eight Habits of the Heart are the building blocks we use, you'll recall, and unselfishness is the mortar that links them all together. The importance of building community and displaying unselfish concern for its members has been a thread connecting chapter to chapter. Now I'd like to take the metaphor one step further and tell you what we build with our blueprint for school community: a Great Wall of Defense against the tyranny of ignorance.

If any wall is to stand and become formidable, its foundation must be deep and solid; that's why following the blueprint for community is so important. But a sturdy wall also must use the strongest materials and the most enduring mortar. We could hardly choose better than the spirit of unselfishness—putting the needs of others ahead of our own—as expressed in the time-tested principles I call the Eight Habits of the Heart: Nurturing Attitude, Responsibility, Dependability, Friendship, Brotherhood, High Expectations, Courage, and Hope.

But no project can be successful without master builders who are knowledgeable, skilled, and motivated to complete the project. And those builders, of course, are you: the educators who are committed to the care of America's future trustees. This book invites you to consider—singly or in groups—the kind of school community where your students can achieve excellence, and where you and your colleagues can thrive as well. With your blueprint in hand, you have an opportunity to embrace, live out, and pass along the life principles that will help hold your school community together.

The Eight Habits of the Heart described here, however, are the building materials not only for today's school communities but for the kind of society we envision in the future. This is the society that the children in today's schools are called upon to build. To accomplish this enormously significant task, they must also develop the Eight Habits of the Heart as they transition from today's students to tomorrow's community trustees. Educators like you must provide them with the model: You must show them how these enduring principles look in real life and the kinds of miracles these habits can perform when they are implemented with a consistently unselfish heart.

You see, then, how important it is for you to adopt the Eight Habits of the Heart and make them part of your own life. Of course, these principles are not entirely new to you. Educators come to their work more or less well equipped with characteristics like Responsibility, Courage, and Hope. To help you assess where you stand today, I have developed the Eight Habits of the Heart Benchmark Chart, provided here.

The Benchmark Chart invites you to give yourself a score on each of the Eight Habits of the Heart, a score between 1 and 8, 8 being what we call a skilled community builder. It is also a tool that educators can use to define the culture of their schools. The growth opportunity provided here doesn't require new tax assessments or budget enhancements. Rather, the freely given actions of individual educators make the difference, build the excellence, erase the fear, and welcome students to their future.

Please take a few minutes, now that you've read the book, and ask yourself about the role these habits of the heart play in your life and where you feel that you are on the chart. Be a tough grader. While the score of 8 doesn't necessarily have to be reserved for the likes of Eleanor Roosevelt, Mary M. Bethune, and Mother Teresa, it should not be awarded lightly. If you are part of a group reading this book, score the culture of your school first, as a group, and discuss your reasons. Then, complete a personal Benchmark Chart, and consider the variance between your assessment of the school and your assessment of yourself. You'll find it to be quite interesting.

Of course, this is not a scientific exercise, but completing the Benchmark Chart will give you a sense of how you have employed these habits so far, and of course, if you reassess yourself from time to time, you'll have a way to visualize your progress. Your movement toward personal unselfishness for the benefit of others, embodied in

Clifton L. Taulbert's

BENCHMARK CHART

P E R S O N A L   A S S E S S M E N T

	1	2	3	4	5	6	7	8
Nurturing Attitude	●	○	○	○	○	○	○	○
Responsibility	●	○	○	○	○	○	○	○
Dependability	●	○	○	○	○	○	○	○
Friendship	●	○	○	○	○	○	○	○
Brotherhood	●	○	○	○	○	○	○	○
High Expectations	●	○	○	○	○	○	○	○
Courage	●	○	○	○	○	○	○	○
Hope	●	○	○	○	○	○	○	○

Apprentice   Journeyman   Skilled

Based upon your understanding of the Eight Habits of the Heart, please indicate your position.

Note: We all start on the "Apprentice" level!

Name: _____   *Date:* _____

these Eight Habits, will ensure the presence of community and strengthen the Great Wall of Defense against the tyranny of ignorance. I think it's important to recall again the words of Dr. John W. Gardner, the great advocate for building community:

> No society can remain vital or even survive without a reasonable base of shared values. Where community exists, it confers upon its members identity, a sense of belonging, a measure of security. A community has the power to motivate its members to exceptional performance. Community can set standards of expectations for the individual and provide the climate in which great things happen.

You the educator must take the lead if we are to create communities within our schools that set high standards for individuals and provide the climate in which "great things happen."

The great things are twofold: great achievements for the students personally and greatness for the society that they grow up to build. Without a Great Wall of Defense, however, their lives might be overcome by negative forces that minimize their intellectual potential and their contributions to society. Your planned and consistent unselfishness and your intentional use of the Eight Habits of the Heart can make all the difference.

I appreciate the opportunity to share with you the world of my youth. In the Mississippi Delta of the 1950s and 1960s, education was my Great Wall of Defense against the tyranny of racism and intimidation. Without my enlightened teachers, I and all the other children of Glen Allan and similar communities might have succumbed to the pressures of our legally segregated world.

Educators who share their wisdom and their commitment are no less needed in today's world. For the benefit of the children now in your presence, and for their children and their children's children, I encourage you to stand at the front door like Miss Maxey and welcome your students into a world where knowledge is imparted, learning takes place, and community binds us all. The legacy of your actions will write the stories of future generations.

Index

**CORWIN
PRESS**

The Corwin Press logo—a raven striding across an open book—
represents the union of courage and learning. Corwin Press is
committed to improving education for all learners by publishing books
and other professional development resources for those serving the
field of PreK–12 education. By providing practical, hands-on materials,
Corwin Press continues to carry out the promise of its motto: **"Helping
Educators Do Their Work Better."**